T0090495

JESUS
AND THE
MANOSPHERE

PAUL TREACY

WESTBOW
PRESS®
A DIVISION OF THOMAS NELSON
& ZONDERVAN

WestBow Press books may be ordered through booksellers or by contacting:

WestBow Press
A Division of Thomas Nelson & Zondervan
1663 Liberty Drive
Bloomington, IN 47403
www.westbowpress.com
844-714-3454

Scripture quotations are taken from the Holy Bible, King James Version.

ISBN: 979-8-3850-0556-7 (sc)
ISBN: 979-8-3850-0557-4 (e)

Library of Congress Control Number: 2023915681

Print information available on the last page.

WestBow Press rev. date: 03/12/2024

CONTENTS

Acknowledgements vii

Preface ix

Introduction.. xi

Part 1   Jesus – His Love And Compassion For
Women.. 1

Part 2   Rise Of The Manosphere 36

Part 3   Can We Ever Go Back To The Way It
Used To Be? 86

Conclusion 143

Extra: Becoming A Christian 161

Acknowledgements

My family, from both near and far. Rufus, Ute Araoye & Family. Keith & Margaret Oliver, Jonathan & Heather Brain, James Gardiner, Nigel Grima, Martyn Brown, Cara Simmens, Keith & Sharon Wilson, Liam Berry & Family, Margaret Woolford, Richard Alvis, Wayne & Marie Innocence Lawther.

Special thanks to:

'Stand to Reason' of Signal Hill, California.
Brett Kunkle of MAVEN, Tustin, California. – Formerly with Stand to Reason.
Reverend Michael Foster of Batavia Ohio.

PREFACE

———◆———

"There is definitely a book in you."

This is something that my Dad would often say to me, throughout my childhood years. I had such a huge imagination as a boy and was great at telling stories and talking in depth about history, geography, astronomy and science – Which were, and still are, among some of my biggest passions. I always thought the idea of myself becoming an author, a truly ludicrous one at the time. Here I was, an awkward and socially inadequate, freckle faced boy from a Wiltshire, council house estate. Unaware I was Autistic. I wasn't involved in any sports and activity groups, like some of the far more popular kids in my neighbourhood were. And it wasn't until the age of twenty-one, during the Summer of 1998, that I travelled anywhere further than northern Germany: the only foreign country I had ever visited up until then, while other classmates went on regular holidays to Spain, Greece and even Florida.

One day, aged around twelve, I went into the local WH Smith, book and stationery supplies store and spotted a couple of books about classic, steam railway engines, which were written by the Reverend Eric Treacy. I had never known anyone with the same, Irish surname as me to have ever written a book before. He had been an avid, railway enthusiast, all of his life and a serving man of God for decades, becoming the Bishop of Pontefract, West Yorkshire and later on, the Bishop of Wakefield, also of West Yorkshire, before retiring. He was called home, while he was waiting for a steam train to arrive on the platform of Appleby train station, Cumbria, north west England in May 1978. His faith and love of steam engines were at the core centre of his life. (No doubt he probably encouraged many people to faith, during his many travels.)

This was also the case for the far more well known, Reverend Wilbert Awdry, the creator of the Thomas the Tank Engine series and who also inspired me to write, along with other renowned authors, such as Roald Dahl and the Reverend, Nicky Gumbel. Reverend Awdry, lived for a while in the village of Box, just six miles from my hometown of Chippenham, where he got the inspiration for his series, observing the steam trains during the day and listening to them passing, close by at night, going in and out of the near two-mile-long, Box Tunnel, built by one of Britain's greatest engineering pioneers, Ismbard Kingdom Brunel. I have always had a love for all things, steam related and have enjoyed numerous such programmes and documentaries over the years, such as the programmes presented by the late, Fred Dibnah.

Deep down, after Reverend Eric Treacy came to my attention, I knew I also had a 'book in me' too. And even possibly more.

INTRODUCTION

———◆———

The passing of Her Majesty, Queen Elizabeth II at Balmoral Castle, Scotland, on September 8th 2022, at aged ninety-six years, was a truly sad day for the British people and for the World. This, despite the fact that we all knew that day we had all been dreading for some time, would soon be upon us. Her reign as Queen, lasted for a record breaking, seventy years: surpassing the previous record held by Queen Victoria, whose reign lasted sixty-four years. Queen Elizabeth II was still a young lady at the time her reign first began in 1952. She was in a remote region of Kenya at the time, when she learned of the passing of her Father, King George VI.

Upon her arrival back to England, she was greeted by then Prime Minister, Sir Winston Churchill. The United Kingdom, as well as much of Europe, was still recovering from the devastation and horrors inflicted by the Nazi regime. Many people had their lives turned upside down and lost loved ones, during those truly, terrible years. And with the new, looming threat of the Soviet Union, under the rule of Josef Stalin, with the beginning of what would be known as the Cold War, then in its early stages, the future seemed very uncertain for all the peoples of Europe at the time and morale would have understandably been low for many. While Queen Elizabeth II obviously was not able to solve all of the World's problems, she certainly played a huge role in reinstalling much needed confidence and morale to the war-scarred nation. As the then, Princess Elizabeth, on her twenty first Birthday in 1947, she gave a long, beautiful and moving speech in which she concluded:

"I declare before you, that my whole life, whether it be long or short, shall be devoted to your service of our great, imperial family to which we all belong. But, I shall not have strength to carry out this resolution alone unless you join in it with me, as I now invite you to do. I know that your support will be unfailingly given. God help me to make good my vow, and God bless you all of you who are willing to share in it."

And how she fulfilled that promise with her kindness, commitment, devotion and love, over the following decades towards the British people and the Commonwealth. From World leaders to everyday people, those who were fortunate enough to have met her, had memories to treasure for the rest of their lives. The only time I ever saw her for myself was when she visited my then workplace: the Dyson, vacuum cleaner factory and research centre in Malmesbury Wiltshire, back in 2001, just weeks before I left there. James Dyson, who later became Knighted, was by her side throughout the visit of the huge facility.

From Sir Winston Churchill to the very brief Prime Minister, Liz Truss, (who met The Queen at Balmoral Castle just two days before her passing) there were a total of fifteen Prime Ministers during her long and glorious reign. She had visited over one hundred countries, met some of the most influential figures modern history, attended countless, historic events in politics, culture, sports, music and the arts, while being patron of countless charities, among which were causes helping vulnerable adults, disabled children and animals. Her Majesty, Queen Elizabeth II, will rightly be remembered as one of the greatest, all–time figures in human history.

During the six–hour long journey that the hearse of Queen Elizabeth II made upon leaving Balmoral Castle, deep in the Scottish countryside of Aberdeenshire, where she passed away, right the way down to Edinburgh, via Aberdeen and Dundee, countless thousands, lined the route along the way and also in villages and towns. Many farmers lined their tractors, side by side and draped them in flags. The crowds, lining the streets of Edinburgh were truly enormous. Many, many more people made their way to London from across Britain, Europe and the whole world, to pay their respects and laid astronomical amounts of flowers and tributes in Green Park, very close to Buckingham Palace, which I went and seen for myself on the following Tuesday after her passing, and I laid down a wee teddy bear that used to belong to my son, Joseph, as a baby. The mountainous flowers and tributes, were a sight to behold. The many, many messages left, were very heart-warming.

After the Queens coffin was flown down to London during the same time I was returning westwards, home to Wiltshire, that same night, thousands lined the streets as the hearse made its way to Buckingham Palace and then the following day from there, in procession to Westminster Hall: the oldest building on Parliament grounds, where the coffin stayed for several days. During that time, many people endured queuing for very long periods of time, some for over eighteen hours, to walk by the coffin within Westminster Hall. The changing of the guard, as is tradition, took place every twenty minutes, with the process lasting three to four minutes each time, prolonging the waiting in the queues. Many who endured being in the very long and exhausting queues, stated categorically, that it was all completely worth it.

The day of the actual funeral on Monday 19th September 2022 was deeply moving, as the coffin was taken from Westminster Hall and placed upon the very same gun carriage used on Queen Victoria's 1901 funeral and which was moved and steered by over one hundred sailors, using the same methods as back then. After reaching Wellington Arch, the coffin was transferred to a hearse for the very final journey to Windsor Castle, twenty-five miles away. Well over one million people lined the route of the final journey with crowds being fifteen to twenty strong on either side of the road as the hearse approached the last 1.5 miles of Windsor Castle. Her final place of rest. It will certainly take a while at this present time to get used to life without her and to get used to the reign of King Charles III and Camilla, The Queen Consort, who for a long time, used to live just under three miles away from my current address at time of writing, in the north Wiltshire countryside. The reign of King Charles III will no doubt be a fairly brief one and many people are looking forward to Prince William, taking to the throne.

The United Kingdom of Great Britain and Northern Ireland, during the reign of Queen Elizabeth II, seen many huge, social and cultural changes, as well as challenges, along the way. Enormous improvements have been made in science, technology and medicine, to name but a few. Greater legislation has been put into place to improve living and working standards and also to combat and punish those who use intimidation and violence towards ethnic minorities and vulnerable people. This country has seen an influx of people from across the world, over the ensuing decades and has welcomed in people from the 'Windrush generation', Jamaican and Caribbean peoples in the 1950s to expelled Ugandan Asians in the early 1970s to Ukrainian refugees in the early 2020s.

But very sadly, during the reign of Queen Elizabeth II, the United Kingdom of Great Britain and Northern

Ireland has seen an ever-rapid decline in morals and standards among many people, which has also been evident among all Western nations. Drink and drug fuelled violence, sex crimes and even murder have blighted nearly all communities to an extent, with towns and city centres often becoming no go zones at weekend nights. Britain has seen widescale rioting and disorder on numerous occasions, over the decades. The London riots of 2011, which were sparked after the justifiable, police shooting and killing of a low-level gangster, were particularly shocking its ferocity, which also seen large scale looting of shops, businesses and even residences, throughout the city. Riots also took place in other English cities such as Birmingham, Bristol and Manchester. I can clearly remember watching live, overhead helicopter footage on the News, of the 'House of Reeves' store in Croydon, south London: a long established, family-owned business dating back to Victorian times (with an adjacent street, even named Reeves Corner, after it) burn into an almighty, huge fireball, within just the space of several minutes. The business has luckily survived in the following years since and they still currently operate from the surviving section of the business, located just across the road from where the main store burned down.

Since the 1960s onwards, violence and sex crimes towards women and children have sharply increased, especially since the advent of the internet into people's homes. Many of those who have been caught in my home

County of Wiltshire and across the United Kingdom in possession of indecent images, were professionals from respectable backgrounds and not that of the typical stereotype, of a scruffy, overweight, middle-aged man of low intelligence, living alone in a squalid apartment. Standards have fallen dramatically too, in regards to the British education system, policing and the judicial system. Our prisons are overcrowded, with drugs and with violence, a growing occurrence. Many crimes go unpunished and/or with criminals given mere, lenient sentences, often because the prisons are at breaking point. In May 2017, my friend Russell, a kindly and humble but very vulnerable man, was brutally killed by someone who was released early from prison for a previous, violent crime against another man. His killing is too graphic to describe.

It was during this very same time, that I could not properly live in my own flat for a considerable while. This situation went on for months because of regular trouble from local yobs and later on, 'County Lines' criminal gangs who took over the flat of my then, vulnerable next-door neighbour. This scourge has affected vulnerable residents and their neighbours in just about every town and city throughout England and Wales, since the early 2010s. Disruptive behaviour, fighting and loud music were of a regular occurrence, with both my neighbour at the time and myself, put at risk of danger on a regular basis, due to the fact many of these gangs arm themselves with weapons, while very little was done by the authorities, until it reached more worsening levels and when more respectable people within the neighbourhood, also started to complain. Those involved in the County Lines scourge are very cowardly and often use children to transport drugs to other towns and cities. Had the authorities dealt with these types of crimes more swiftly, the way they would have done back in the 1950s, when Queen Elizabeth II was in the early years of her reign, then the chances are that Russell would still be alive and my neighbourhood situation and that of thousands of others, would have been dealt with more very quickly and efficiently. My ex-neighbours flat was terribly damaged once an eviction notice was issued and as far as I know, nobody was ever arrested for what happened there, during that time. Uber liberal attitudes towards crime, such as these, make an absolute mockery of what used to be the greatest Police and Justice system, known in the world with ever more increasing, 'red tape', hindering what officers are able to do when dealing with criminals and with many such criminals, often laughing at the law. Powers of 'stop and search' for knives and weapons, come under regular criticism from uber left wing, 'social justice warriors', who feel that officers are 'picking on' ethnic youths. This, despite the fact that they are trying to stop stabbings and killings, which are common in particular, among that demographic, within inner-city boroughs. The annual, policing budget that is spent each year on more meaningless, 'non-jobs', useless 'diversity' courses and feelgood schemes, would be much better spent, funding many more Policemen and women on the streets, to help to keep our communities safer. Many Officers are often held to their desks, having to deal with too much, time consuming paperwork and seeing Officers on the beat these days is a rarity, with the exception of Central London.

My Dad described that back in the 1950s and some of the 1960s, the main 'Bobby' (Policeman) on the beat in the Chippenham area, was a battle hardened, World War Two veteran who stood at 6'4ft tall and who was both feared and respected by everyone in town. Any local drunk he arrested, soon sobered up quick! It was hardly surprising, that the crime rate was so low in the town back then, which, at the time, had more public houses than in this current era. Now, whenever I watch Policing documentaries, with 5'7ft tall Officers, sporting hipster beards, who are literally de facto, social workers, being out of their depth, while trying to deal with alcohol and cocaine fuelled thugs, spilling out of nightclubs in the early hours, I truly despair and think of how the Bobbies of yesteryear would have handled such situations. All such thugs would have been punished far more severely. (Around 25% of current, serving UK Police officers would not have made it into the force by pre-1990 standards. Hundreds of whom, have also been found to have been truly unpleasant and predatory characters.) Like all sane thinking people, I absolutely despair at the sight of Police Officers dancing along with revellers at gay pride parades and seeing Police cars emblazoned with rainbow flags. Close to my area, Avon and Somerset Police Officers held an event where male Officers could apply make-up on themselves and have their fingernails painted red to help 'celebrate diversity.' There were similar events in numerous, other forces, across the country. An absolute embarrassment that makes a mockery of British Policing. Along with millions of fed-up Britons, I personally, bear no grudge against our good and honest Policemen and women, some of whom have encountered life threatening dangers at some stage or another, during the course of their careers. It is the very out of touch hierarchy, in their Central London bubble, who make life harder for regular Bobbies and who orchestrate this continuous 'woke' nonsense, all of this, while robberies, burglaries and sex crimes surge, year on year.

What exactly has happened since the early 1950s, when Queen Elizabeth II first took to the throne, to lead us to the absolute mess, where we are now? Many such British people at the time, and men in particular, who served, fighting Germany and Italy in Europe and North Africa, and Japanese forces in south east Asia in the previous decade, would have loved to have had just half of what many of us now take for granted. The average, UK life expectancy rates, up until the 1960s for both men and women, was around 62-65 years, with a great deal of people, often dying in discomfort for various reasons. However, despite the fact many young men and women endured terrible horrors and lost friends during battle, many hundreds of thousands of surviving, World War Two veterans were actually fortunate enough to have the love and unwavering support of good women and enjoy marriages that often lasted for fifty years or more, while also enjoying a far better quality of life than their own parents had, raising happy children and living healthy and productive lives, throughout. (This was sadly, far less common for World War One survivors, most of whom, returned to dire poverty and who were far more prone to life changing injuries and the debilitating condition known as 'shell shock' – involving, violent, involuntary jolting and spasms of the limbs and who often died earlier from other health conditions faced during the absolute horrors of trench warfare.)

During this current, modern era, with improvements over the decades in healthcare, better standards of food, water, sanitation and standards of living, average UK, life expectancy rates are now around 79–82 years of age, with more people than ever before in British history, now living beyond ninety years of age. Millions of current Britons, live in a warm home, own a car and get to travel abroad, once or twice a year. More reasons to be cheerful then? To be happier and content with our lot in life? Very sadly, for so many people, this is simply not the case. Along with the decline of Christian beliefs and values, combined with the sexual revolution of the 1960s, the traditional, family unit has also come under great attack over the subsequent decades with far greater divorce rates and break ups than ever before, combined with the huge rise of single parent families. While there are many absent fathers who should be brought to task if they try to avoid paying any form of child support, there are also many good fathers out there who are denied access to their children, through the family court system, with a percentage of ex-wives who 'weaponize' their children, in order to be as spiteful as possible. Children without a father in their lives and not raised in a healthy, loving home are, in adult life, far more likely to lead blighted and dysfunctional lives. While some people in politics, entertainment, movies and sports, have managed to rise through the ranks, while being raised in single parent households, they are among the very slim exception to the statistics and not the norm.

Marriage rates, along with children born in wedlock, continue to decline, while marriage rates in most, Muslim majority countries, continue to rise. It is now getting to the very stage, since the mid-2010s, where so many young men are not even able to forge relationships at all. Chronic loneliness is now becoming a very concerning issue, also giving rise to alcoholism, drug abuse, gambling issues/debts and more mental health issues. An average of twelve men, who are of all ages, take their own lives in Great Britain every single day – Amounting to over four thousand, every year. These statistics, combined with the current, cost of living crisis at this time of writing, with job insecurity in many sectors, is also another factor. Very sadly, suicide rates will continue to rise. Many, young men, more than ever, are now feeling alienated and disillusioned with life, where they feel that society – and indeed, many women – neither care for them nor value them. They are far more likely to feel more that way if they come from lower, socio-economic backgrounds.

Now, among this looming turmoil and despair, a fast growing movement and subculture known as the 'manosphere' (Also commonly referred to as the 'red pill movement') has grown from strength to strength, and in which, among its core beliefs, firmly believes that 'toxic feminism' and warped, ultra-left 'woke' attitudes, have seeped into just about, all of our institutions, which are destroying them from within and are also slowly destroying the traditional, family unit, thus continually making life more and more harder for decent, everyday men - And it is now slowly, beginning to rot our entire, Western civilisation from the inside out. Those within the manosphere strongly believe that this 'enemy within' poses an even greater threat to Western civilisation than Al-Qaeda and the Islamic State movement. The main, leading figures within the current movement have large, global followings online, with one Mr Andrew Tate in particular, who holds some deeply controversial views, has often been given bizarre labels, such as the 'King of the manosphere' and the 'King of misogyny', having at one time, had his name searched on Google more often, than the former, American President, Donald Trump and the global reality star, Kim Kardashian. The often deeply controversial, manosphere movement claims to be a 'brotherhood', in which as well as offering advice on lifestyle and relationships and with helping men to 'learn game' and to 'understand how women think and react', while also giving advice on looking smart, on fitness, nutrition, business and financial advice, which also includes cryptocurrencies such as Bitcoin, in some quarters. I have searched extensively online and to date, have not seen any other Christian book author who has touched upon the subject of the manosphere, although it is only a matter of time before someone would eventually do so.

Another reason why the life and passing of Her Majesty, Queen Elizabeth II was so profound to the British people, The Commonwealth and much of the wider world, was her devotion to her family. Her strong, Christian faith helped to develop the strength with the family unit, which so many of us wished we could have had in our own families in both our childhood and adult years. Despite the tough challenges, The Royal Family have faced over the years, such the death of Princess Diana in Paris France in 1997, the now strained relationship with Prince Harry and Princess Meghan and of course, Prince Andrew's associations with Jeffrey Epstein and the socialite, Ghislaine Maxwell, the youngest daughter of the disgraced media tycoon, Robert Maxwell, which a small hardcore of anti-royalists are always keen to remind us of, (not that we needed reminding) the long and glorious reign of Queen Elizabeth II, is almost certain never to be surpassed, anywhere in the future, by anyone else, ever.

Many of us can learn from the reign of Queen Elizabeth II, especially young women and girls, growing up in an ever increasing, sexualised and materialistic world, which in turn is often very damaging to them. Please be warned that much of the following content within, is of a sensitive and sexual nature, which may make for uncomfortable reading for some people. However, such discussions and topics need to be faced and examined thoroughly and not to be swept under the carpet. To ignore and dismiss such concerning issues would be a great folly indeed. We do so at our peril.

PART ONE

JESUS – HIS LOVE AND COMPASSION FOR WOMEN

———◆———

The society and culture in Palestine during the First Century AD, was a fundamentally, patriarchal one, as was the Roman Empire which occupied the territories at the time. Though Jesus did indeed have twelve, all male disciples, a great deal of the New Testament talks about his encounters with women. Jesus was of course, born to Mary in a manger in Bethlehem and he had immense love and respect for his Mother. And we see throughout the New Testament that Jesus loved and cared for all women and girls that he met, also healing and comforting many on his travels, including those women who were deeply scorned and shunned by society, such as prostitutes and beggars. Never once, does Jesus become rude and unpleasant towards any of the women he meets, unlike many of the men of the time, whose casually abusive behaviour, would have made the lives of such women, much more difficult to bear. Among the many women he healed, was a woman who suffered with continual, menstrual bleeding, lasting twelve years. She simply touched his garment as he was walking by and Jesus had stopped to ask who had touched him. This, despite the fact that there was a large crowd present. The woman trembled at his feet and explained why she touched him.

> [32] And he looked round about to see her that had done this thing.
> [33] But the woman fearing and trembling, knowing what was done in her, came and fell down before him, and told him all the truth.
> [34] And he said unto her, Daughter, thy faith hath made thee whole; go in peace, and be whole of thy plague.
> (Mark 5: 32–34 KJV)

From Wikipedia: 'Jesus treated her as having worth, not rebuking her for what the Levitical code of holiness would have considered as defiling him. Rather, he relieved her of any sense of guilt for her seemingly rash act, lifted her up and called her 'daughter.' He told her that her faith had saved her, gave her his love, and sent her away whole.' (Mark 5: 25–34) Jesus showed kindness to the woman at the well when she saw no value in herself. (John 4: 1–42) He rebuked the disciples and defended the woman who poured expensive perfume on his head, honouring her faith and humility. (Mark 14: 1–11) and (Luke 7: 36–50) Jesus also helped a woman who couldn't walk upright to stand up straight again. (Luke 13: 10–17) And, he healed the Mother in law of Simon Peter, his most cherished disciple, who was bedridden with a fever – As mentioned three times in the New Testament. Jesus also raised the deceased daughter of Jarius, one of the rulers of the Jewish synagogue, back to life. And of course, Jesus saved the life of an adulterous woman who was about to be stoned.

> 'So when they continued asking him, he lifted up himself, and said unto them, He that is without sin among you, let him first cast a stone at her.' (John 8:7 KJV)

In many of his sermons and parables, women were regularly mentioned.

And, as the bloodied and scourged Jesus was forced to carry his own cross, many women and girls would have lined the route, with most of them probably crying and wailing uncontrollably. As he was nailed to the cross and as it was put into place, his Mother Mary, her Sister, Mary of Clopas and Mary Magdalene, were present. John is the only disciple, present at the crucifixion. It is highly likely that many hundreds of women, would have come and gone in the hours that Jesus was nailed to the cross to see him and the two thieves, who were also crucified, either side of him. It is also highly likely, that women would have outnumbered the men who witnessed it.

After his death and being taken down from the cross, the body of Jesus was placed in a tomb with a large stone circle, rolled in front of the entrance. Jesus returned to life that following Sunday and Mary Magdalene was the very first person to have seen the resurrected Jesus, followed by other women. There would have been a great deal of women who would have seen Jesus during those forty days that he remained on Earth before his ascension into Heaven. The resurrection of Jesus is the most significant event in the history of mankind. Jesus, conquered the grave – And women were the first to witness it. This, in a society where they were regarded as being among the least important of people. (With the exception of those married to high ranking, Roman officials.) Let that sink in for a moment. It is hardly surprising then, that over the centuries, countless women, the entire world over, including those not raised in Christian households, have turned to Jesus – And with many helping the poor, playing a role in positive, historic events from the abolition of slavery to social reforms in hospitals, schools, prisons and much more. Many such women have also played a unique and vital role in encouraging other women and indeed, even men, to faith.

Any true man, anywhere in the world will love and want to protect their mothers, sisters, daughters and female relatives, if they too have treated them with love, dignity and respect over the years, in return. Even men with a serious 'reputation', ranging from the often lively, Liam and Noel Gallagher of the Oasis, Britpop band fame, to the even more fearsome, Ronald and Reginald Kray: the infamous twin brothers who ruled the East End of London through fear and violence during the

1950s and 1960s. Both sets of brothers, in spite of the fact they were far from angelic, have a very deep love for their mothers. As for me, I could not have asked for a more fantastic mother than my own, Aberdeen born and raised mother, who has overcome some tough challenges herself, through the years.

As with any sane and rational thinking person, I truly hate and despise anything that involves violence and crimes of a sexual nature by men, towards women and children, especially girls, anywhere on Earth: from women and girls being murdered in so called 'honour' killings and being victims of acid attacks on the Indian subcontinent. Of young women, being forced to wear the all covering, burqa veil in Afghanistan and being beaten, should they remove it in public. Of girls being forced to endure the horrific and sometimes fatal practice of female genital mutilation (FGM) in Somalia and of the mass scale murders and rapes of women and girls, that have taken place over the decades, throughout much of the rest of African continent, especially in regions of civil war and unrest. From Mexico to Brazil, there are often high rates of female murders due to high levels of domestic violence and of women and girls ending up as 'collateral damage' in brutal, gun battles: from small time gangsters to major cartels, fighting for control and territory in the multi-billion, international drugs trade.

One of toughest films I ever watched, was 'The Magdalene Sisters': a factual play, which is set in the

Republic of Ireland, during the early 1960s, which shown how truly horrendous the lives were, for the so called 'fallen women', who were sent to institutions, supported by the state and run by the Catholic Church. Those who were in charge of the institutions were brutal and sadistic nuns, who also lived there and who took pleasure in their ungodly treatment. Priests would visit occasionally and also mete out abuse. The women sent there were forced to clean laundry for local hotels for hours each day and without being paid for it. Although most of the women were sent there for having babies outside of wedlock, (with many babies being adopted by American and Canadian couples) some women were sent there for the flimsiest of reasons. One of the main characters in the film, a pretty teenage girl called Bernadette, was sent to the institution after some of her teachers were 'concerned' at her flirting with local boys who turned up and started to whistle at her on the other side of the railings of the school playground she was at, during her lunch break. It is estimated that as many as 30,000 women ended up in such institutions over the years and which only closed for good in the mid-1990s.

Violence, brutality and sexual abuse towards women and girls is never acceptable in any shape or form. The anger it can quell within someone is perfectly understandable, but which in turn can make some seek bloodthirsty revenge. In the Old Testament, the daughter of King David, Tamar, is raped by her half-brother, Amnon, as he pretended to be physically unwell and as she tended to help him. (2 Samuel: 13.) He claimed to be 'madly in love' with her but had total hatred and contempt for her, thereafter. King David, despite his anger, refuses to have Amnon put to death, much to the fury of Absolom, Tamar's full-blooded brother. Two years later, during a feast, Absolom orders his servants to kill Amnon, after he became drunk with wine. This was to then set the wheels in motion for a civil war, with Absolom laying claim to the throne and with the people and armies torn between their loyalty to King David and Absolom. During the Battle of the wood of Ephraim, as Absolom's loyalists were losing, Absolom then fled on horseback. In a freak accident, he ended up being suspended from the sticky branches of a tree by his long hair as his horse ran underneath the tree and kept on running. Despite being ordered by his Father, King David, to spare the life of his son if his loyalists were overthrown, his commander Joab struck Absolom dead with his spear as he dangled helplessly, from the tree.

King David was warned years before by the prophet Nathan, that evil would be raised against him from his own house. This, after caving in to his lustful feelings for the beautiful and married, Bathsheba, whom he had seen, living a very short distance from one of his palace balconies. He summoned her and engaged in an adulterous relationship with Bathsheba and with King David impregnating her. King David had then ordered Bathsheba's soldier husband, Uriah, to return to the palace to give a report of how the battle was going, and then asked him to stay a few days, in the hope that he would go home to his wife and make love to her, believing that the baby she was carrying in her womb, would be his own. Instead, he camped outside the palace, telling King David that it would be wrong to be in his marital bed at night when his comrades could not do the same with their own wives. King David also got Uriah drunk, on another evening, during his time of leave, in the hope that he would 'loosen up' and return to his wife. But he still refused to do so. On the day Uriah was due to return to the military camp, Uriah was asked by King David to give the battle commander, Joab, a scrolled message, in which King David ordered that Uriah was to be placed at the heat of the next battle, at the front, where he would most likely be killed. And he was. Bathsheba lost her baby at birth, just as the prophet Nathan had prophesized.

Nathan Rebukes David (2 Samuel: 12, 1-14 KJV.)

> And the Lord sent Nathan unto David. And he came unto him, and said unto him, There were two men in one city; the one rich, and the other poor.
> 2 The rich man had exceeding many flocks and herds:
> 3 But the poor man had nothing, save one little ewe lamb, which he had bought and nourished up: and it grew

up together with him, and with his children; it did eat of his own meat, and drank of his own cup, and lay in his bosom, and was unto him as a daughter.

⁴ And there came a traveller unto the rich man, and he spared to take of his own flock and of his own herd, to dress for the wayfaring man that was come unto him; but took the poor man's lamb, and dressed it for the man that was come to him.

⁵ And David's anger was greatly kindled against the man; and he said to Nathan, As the Lord liveth, the man that hath done this thing shall surely die:

⁶ And he shall restore the lamb fourfold, because he did this thing, and because he had no pity.

⁷ And Nathan said to David, Thou art the man. Thus saith the Lord God of Israel, I anointed thee king over Israel, and I delivered thee out of the hand of Saul;

⁸ And I gave thee thy master's house, and thy master's wives into thy bosom, and gave thee the house of Israel and of Judah; and if that had been too little, I would moreover have given unto thee such and such things.

⁹ Wherefore hast thou despised the commandment of the Lord, to do evil in his sight? thou hast killed Uriah the

Hittite with the sword, and hast taken his wife to be thy wife, and hast slain him with the sword of the children of Ammon.

¹⁰ Now therefore the sword shall never depart from thine house; because thou hast despised me, and hast taken the wife of Uriah the Hittite to be thy wife. ¹¹ Thus saith the Lord, Behold, I will raise up evil against thee out of thine own house, and I will take thy wives before thine eyes, and give them unto thy neighbour, and he shall lie with thy wives in the sight of this sun.

¹² For thou didst it secretly: but I will do this thing before all Israel, and before the sun.

¹³ And David said unto Nathan, I have sinned against the Lord. And Nathan said unto David, The Lord also hath put away thy sin; thou shalt not die.

¹⁴ Howbeit, because by this deed thou hast given great occasion to the enemies of the Lord to blaspheme, the child also that is born unto thee shall surely die.

King David later admitted to Bathsheba about his plot for Uriah's demise, which angered the Lord who then took their baby. She in turn would admit, that her adultery had also played a part in the death of her husband and baby son. King David eventually married Bathsheba and she later bore him Solomon, who would eventually succeed King David later on, to the throne.

Woman.
How much blood's been shed over a woman.
How much moneys spent out on a woman.
Ever since the dawn of man.
Yeah.
A woman.

Woman.
Nations rise and fall over a woman.
Even kings will cry before a woman.
Ever since the dawn of man.
Yeah.
A woman.

First two verses of 'Woman' by Lady Blackbird.

Almighty God, who created the Universe and this Earth, has an immense love for men and boys, women and girls, the entire world over, though he abhors sin and sexual sin in particular, very deeply. As seen in the case of King David, such actions can lead to very dire and tragic consequences. He already had numerous wives and lived in great luxury but his lustful desires had got the better of him, which would lead to two innocent deaths and much more, further trouble among his own family, in the following years to come. Hence, the importance of strong faith, marriage and the family unit: which is the foundation of any true, functioning society. Jesus also died a very cruel death upon the cross for our sins, our rebelliousness and lustful desires. He died for all women and girls in equal measure to men and boys. Jesus even died on the cross, for the worst of female killers, such as Myra Hindley and Aileen Wuornos, just as much as he did, for the most well-known, influential, pioneering women in history, such as Marie Curie and Florence Nightingale. God wants us to turn away from our sin and towards him, to eventually marry and raise decent, loving children, if we haven't already done so. And furthermore, for us to lead the best lives possible. Love and marriage has always been an integral part of humanity and culture.

However, something has happened in recent decades in our own Western culture: Marriages and relationships have rapidly declined. There are more divorces and break ups, and it is harder to start and grow relationships than ever before....And yet, we now live far more comfortable lives, can travel and communicate with each other, far better than what was actually possible for the huge majority of people at the beginning of the twentieth century. Despite this, most people during those times, were married and had settled down after they reached their mid-twenties. What exactly is going on here? And, therefore, it is time to focus on the ever growing, manosphere movement, which regularly examines these often, complicated issues and which tries to answer these kinds of questions. What is it about exactly and what do they hope to achieve? Is the movement, as many feminists, both moderate and radical, and much of the mainstream media suggest, just a ragtag of sexist and misogynist, bullies and misfits, who insist that women should be conditioned into being compliant, 'Stepford Wives' in order to please them and to bow to their each to every whim? Or is there actually more to it than many people, actually realise? Are there elements within the movement which are in fact, very reasonable and whose viewpoints should be strongly taken into consideration? And we need to ask the biggest question on the subject: What would Jesus himself, ultimately make of the movement? There is no denying that the manosphere movement, which is believed by many to have first begun slowly during the late 1980s to the early 1990s, does have less than savoury and controversial elements within its branches, which cannot be denied and which need to be examined first. As someone who was often on the receiving end of very unpleasant vitriol and abuse, while growing up through the years: some of which was described in my previous, 'Hidden Disabilities' book, I know only too well, how such abuse can be painful and damaging. I do not agree with any hateful and misogynist, online abuse, made by fringe elements within any branches of the movement and I never, ever support violence and intimidation towards women and girls or anyone else.

ELLIOTT RODGER:
TERROR IN CALIFORNIA

On May 23 2014, a disturbed young man, Elliott Rodger, aged 22, the London born son of the British, Hollywood film producer, Peter Rodger, went on a killing rampage in Isla Vista, California, using knives, guns and his own car, to strike at people. He killed six people and injured fourteen more before crashing into a parked car and shooting himself dead, just moments before the local police, closed in on him. Elliott had been planning his attack for a considerable time, while writing a detailed 'manifesto' and recording a video beforehand to explain his actions. Elliott was an 'incel': A term meaning 'involuntary celibate.' In short, this is an online community of disenfranchised, young men, who feel that they are unable to forge relationships with young ladies, as they seem to have no interest in them. And, it is for this reason, that Elliott felt a very deep hatred towards those women who had turned him down. And then later on, a deep hatred towards just about all women and girls, which he talked about in previous videos that he had uploaded.

Elliott Rodger strongly believed that, because he was in his own opinion, very handsome (which he wasn't) and that because his Father was a leading figure in the Hollywood industry, being the assistant director to the 2012 'Hunger Games' movie, he felt that women should be flocking to him in their droves. But instead, the 'Stacy's': the most attractive girls, were more interested in the 'Chad's', who were physically strong, very confident and handsome. (The black equivalent of Chad's are referred to as 'Tyrone's'.) Elliott made many ridiculous ramblings and bizarrely referred to himself as being the 'supreme gentleman.' Very sadly, Elliott had struggled with emotional and behavioural difficulties, going back to his earliest, childhood years, while also being regularly bullied and rejected among other children. He made numerous videos on YouTube, during the last two years of his life, spouting his anger and hate towards society as well as to women, while also having bitter hatred towards black and Asian men. The white women who would date such guys, Elliott considered such young women to be the lowest of the low. This, despite of the fact that his own mother was of Chinese-Malaysian origin.

Elliott Rodger has since been viewed as a 'martyr' among the ever growing, incel communities online and on chat forums, across the world. And very sadly, there have been numerous, violent incel attacks in the years since, such as the van attacker in Toronto Canada, in which Alek Minassian, deliberately struck innocent pedestrians and which involved the deaths of ten people and injuring another fifteen more. (An eleventh victim, later succumbed to their injuries in 2021.) The attacker wrote in similar, online ramblings: "We will overthrow the Chad's and Stacy's! All hail the supreme gentleman, Elliott Rodger!" Great Britain was to have its very own, incel killer in the city of Plymouth in southwest England, in August 2021, with Jake Davison, 22, first shooting his mother, then shooting and killing four others including a small girl and injuring two others, before turning his rifle on himself. Jake also made regular, online tirades against what he perceived to be, as life being completely 'rigged' against him and those similar to him, from the day he was born. Across the other side of England in Middlesbrough, in the previous the year, a young man was arrested and later jailed for plotting a violent, incel attack, with explosives and weapons found at his home. Incel forums are often teeming with newer members on a regular basis, with many becoming normalised to 'discussions' about violence, rape and murder.

The earliest known, incel murder, dates back to December 1989, before the term incel was even coined, in Montreal Canada. Marc Lepine, armed with a rifle and hunting knife, entered the Ecole Polytechnique de Montreal, (also referred to as Montreal Polytechnic) killing fourteen people and injuring another fourteen, before more turning his rifle on himself. In a leaked, suicide letter he blamed feminism for ruining his life, his future prospects and Canadian society as a whole. (Due to their more extreme views and beliefs, many people often tend to view the incel movement as being a completely separate entity from the manosphere movement altogether.) As well as incels, there are the 'pick up artists' (PUA's) also known as dating coaches. Some of whom have or have had at one time, a sizeable online following, with many such PUA's holding seminars and conferences, with entry fees often reaching into hundreds of pounds/dollars. Many of their views and some of the techniques that they advise to lonely and frustrated, young men, when it comes to approaching and talking to young women, have been viewed as being bullying, controlling and manipulating, with some PUA's even gaining the attention of anti-hate organisations, along with the online, incel communities. Among their techniques, are acts known as 'negging' and 'progressive touching':

Negging (derived from the verb *neg*, meaning "negative feedback") is an act of emotional manipulation whereby a person makes a deliberate, backhanded compliment or otherwise flirtatious remark to another person to undermine their confidence and increase their need of the manipulator's approval. (Wiki)

Progressive touching, also known as 'kino escalation', is to get physical from the very beginning, in meeting someone new, usually on a first date: starting with genteel, very brief touching of the shoulders and/or waist then very gradually touching the lady more, over the course of 2-3 hours with hugs, a kiss or two and becoming more sexual after that, to test what the man can/cannot get away with. Along with incels and pick up artists, are the Men's Rights Activists: (MRAs) a collection of organisations who believe, among other things, that the state in western nations, often have an unfair bias in favour of women, especially in regards to family courts and employment laws. One of the most well-known groups is 'A Voice For Men' (AVFM) founded by Texan truck driver, Paul Elam in 2009, who has since gained a sizable following over the years. Britain has similar groups, such as 'Fathers 4 Justice' (F4J) by men who have been denied access to their children by the courts. For a time, they held high profile demonstrations, while dressed as superheroes, even managing to breach security at Buckingham Palace and climbing on to the roof, while displaying banners to highlight their cause. They have even climbed up one of the support towers of the Clifton Suspension Bridge in Bristol and have also brought motorways to a halt, in their protests. There is also the group 'Justice For Men And Boys', (J4MB) founded by Mike Buchanan.

Then there is 'Men Going Their Own Way' or MGTOW for short, whose beliefs are that it is best not to engage in any long-term relationships altogether, as they are ultimately doomed to failure because of the scourge of modern feminism, playing a huge role in destroying relationships, the traditional, family unit and that the family and divorce court system, leans heavily in favour of women, regardless of their own behaviour and lifestyle. This, they believe, has led many millions of men, most of whom were decent husbands and who remain as good fathers, to financial ruin and in some cases, suicide.

Many people within the entire spectrum of the manosphere and the millions of followers of the mainstream movement, describe themselves as being 'red pilled.' This, is in reference to a scene in the 1999, science fiction/action film 'The Matrix', in which the main character, Neo, (Keanu Reeves) is offered the choice between a red pill or blue pill by Morpheus. (Laurence Fishburne)

"You take the blue pill, the story ends, you wake up in your bed and believe what you want to believe. You take the red pill.....You stay in wonderland and I will show you how deep the rabbit hole goes." Neo takes the red pill, which shows that hard truth and reality than the blissful ignorance that the blue pill offers. This is actually very similar to what is written in the Bible.

> [13] Enter ye in at the strait gate: for wide is the gate, and broad is the way, that leadeth to destruction, and many there be which go in thereat:
> [14] Because strait is the gate, and narrow is the way, which leadeth unto life, and few there be that find it. (Matthew 7: 13-14 KJV.)

Men who claim to be red pilled, claim to be awakened to what they believe is a world fast becoming scarred by woke and feminist ideologies: unlike the blue pilled men, who are deeply despised by those in the manosphere, with such men often referred to as 'simps' and 'cucks'. These are the easily led, weak men who, if they are in a relationship, are usually with a 'Karen': a bizarre term to describe a bullying and manipulating woman, who, if married, have little or no respect for their husband. These simp husbands will often go above and beyond for their wives, spoiling her with holidays, gifts and treats on a regular basis, living up to the 'happy wife, happy life' motto. However, despite their valiant efforts and best intentions, they will gain very little in return. Many such men are often brought up in unloving homes. They are in many cases, often disrespected by their peers, any ex-wives and any children they may have in any past and/or present relationships.

Exactly why the name Karen was chosen, to describe an unpleasant woman, remains a mystery and there are numerous theories to this online. I have met numerous ladies, named Karen, over the years, who are very pleasant and easy going. A once, innocuous name, now has a ghastly stigma, attached to it. It is highly unlikely that many baby girls will be named Karen in the foreseeable future and that the name will gradually fizzle out, over time.

Why then, do so many men – And even many women, surprisingly enough, with 'red pilled', female, manosphere supporters, like the very popular, online blogger, Pearl Davis: host of the 'Just Pearly Things' podcast and organisations such as the all–female, 'Honey

Badger Brigade', point much of the blame of their woes and breakdown of society, towards modern feminism in particular? Aren't there more pressing issues to focus on? There are looming worries, affecting millions of people on issues such as economic uncertainty, poverty, crime, immigration and the current, war in Ukraine: the ripple effect of which, is having an impact on the global stock market. Surely, all of feminism has been an absolute force for good in the world? What harm could the feminism movement, have ever caused? Are those who make such claims, just bitter and deluded? All decent people, rightfully want to see a better world, plus equality and better opportunities for our daughters and granddaughters. So, what exactly seems to be the problem then?

FEMINISM THROUGH THE YEARS

For much of the second half of the twentieth century, here in Britain, life for so many women were a daily nightmare, regardless of the fact that the overwhelming majority of them were easily able to have three meals a day and a roof, over their heads. Us Britons often refer to this era as being 'Life on Mars', after the BBC comedy/drama, (named after the iconic, David Bowie song) where a detective, after surviving a near fatal car accident, is somehow transported back in time to the 1970s and who is shocked at just how normalised, that misogynist and chauvinist attitudes were, even among the average man on the street. On a serious level, I cannot even begin to imagine how truly horrible and crushing it must have been for the thousands of young ladies, mostly aged under thirty, who worked as secretaries and receptionists, among other female majority positions, in Britain, from the late 1950s, right through to the early 1990s. From the moment they heard the clacking of typewriters and smelled the looming, cigarette smoke, many such young ladies, would no doubt get sinking feelings in their stomachs, hoping and praying that the day ahead would not be one of 'those days.' It had nothing to do with the amount of paperwork, waiting for them upon the 'in-tray' on their desks, but of the predatory nature of some of their bosses and/or male colleagues, some of whom would sexually harass and belittle their female staff on a regular basis, while dismissing it all as merely being workplace banter. (You couldn't report such things to the police at the time, as it would be highly likely that they would not be interested in such complaints.)

Those poor women, who had to rely on public transport to get to work and back, would probably have to face an even longer ordeal and would regularly run the gauntlet of having to endure unpleasant men on board. Many such young women, still living at home, would regularly see their fathers and brothers, roaring with laughter, watching over sexualised, televised 'comedies' such as 'On the Buses' – A play about the regular scrapes of two double decker bus drivers from London, who regularly flirted and slept with, female customers: many of whom were married and young enough to be their own daughters. It is reassuring to know that most young women under thirty in modern, 2020s Britain, have not endured as much as one quarter of what their grandmother's generation had to go through, day in, day out. Sexual harassment and intimidation were literally normalised in many working cultures, back in those times.

Although a great deal of progress has been made since the start of the twenty-first century to combat the scourge of sexist behaviour and unpleasant attitudes, which can often lead to violence against women and girls, there is undoubtedly, still a long way to go in regards to such issues and on how to drastically reduce sexual crimes against women and children.

From Wikipedia:

*The **Everyday Sexism Project** is a website founded on 16 April 2012 by Laura Bates, a British feminist writer. The aim of the site is to document examples of sexism from around the world. Entries may be submitted directly to the site, or by email or tweet. The accounts of abuse are collated by a small group of volunteers. The launch of this website is considered to be the beginning of fourth-wave feminism.*

After graduating from Cambridge University with a degree in English Literature, Bates worked as a nanny and found that the young girls she looked after were already preoccupied with their body image. She set up the Everyday Sexism Project in April 2012 after finding it difficult to speak out about sexism.

Nearly a year after beginning the website, Bates reflected on the common response she had received. "Again, and again, people told me sexism is no longer a problem – that women are equal now, more or less, and if you can't take a joke or take a compliment, then you need to stop being so 'frigid' and get a sense of humour", she told Anna Klassen of The Daily Beast website in April 2013. "Even if I couldn't solve the problem right away, I was determined that nobody should be able to tell us we couldn't talk about it anymore."

Since the project started, Ms Bates, who has since become an accomplished, feminist author, has been overwhelmed with countless, thousands of messages from women and girls, many from across the world, telling of some of the often-appalling treatment they have faced by men and even boys in schools and leisure settings, much of which has been normalised and spurred on because of certain cultures and influences, including from television, social media and aspects of the downmarket, tabloid media. (Ms Bates has herself, very sadly, endured countless vile taunts and threats, over the years.) These in turn, combined with the sexual revolution and the rapid decline of Christianity in everyday, British and Western life, has played a very large role in why most of the second half of the twentieth century, eventually became incredibly seedy and unpleasant. The echoes of which, still continues to this very day.

In the wake of the Jimmy Savile scandals, when the world discovered, one year after his death in October 2011, that this seemingly, selfless, TV and radio entertainer and tireless, charity fundraiser was in fact, one of the most prolific, sex offenders in all of British history, who used his fame and power to intimidate his hundreds of often, vulnerable victims, which also included adults and boys, into silence. In the following years since those horrifying revelations, there has been far greater awareness, understanding and support for survivors of childhood, sexual abuse and adult survivors of rape and sexual violence. For men and boys as well as women and girls. Tackling the scourge of domestic and sexual violence by the criminal justice system in much of the aforementioned matters has improved in more recent years but there is still a long way to go.

Many people, including dozens of renowned, television and radio presenters, used to mock and berate the art teacher turned staunch, Christian activist, Mary Whitehouse, who appeared on numerous, television and radio talk shows to complain about the rising, sexualisation of teenage girls and violence on British television screens, which was also beginning to creep into television channels, during daytime hours. It would be fair to say that Ms Whitehouse was right in so many instances, during her decades of campaigning. It is hardly surprising then, that vulgar and innuendo filled 'Carry on' style films and numerous, similar comedies, like 'On the buses', which were commonplace in the late 1960s, 1970s and 1980s, are no longer made in this current day and age, though I would certainly not advocate for them to be banned outright from our screens, provided they were shown after 8pm.

The annual 'Miss World' event, a somewhat 'grey area' in this debate, was withdrawn from British television screens after 1984, after much complaints and protests from feminists at the time, who felt the contest 'objectified' women and their bodies. This, despite the fact that the show was very popular among both men and women and there were no stories of the contestants ever being exploited, mistreated or abused in any way. Indeed, these women, willingly participated and they freely admitted that they enjoyed the experiences, the contest offered them, combined with the opportunities to travel, better their lives and that of their families. (The 1970 event, hosted at the Royal Albert Hall in London, was hijacked by feminists, who threw bags of flour and rotten fruit and chanted slogans, in order to disrupt it completely. They briefly, brought the event to a halt but were ejected from the Hall by security staff and the contest went on that night, with the first ever black female, crowned Miss World in the contests history – However, the protesting feminists, made their mark, gaining huge media attention for their actions, and it was hailed as a victory for them.) Beauty contests, which for a time, were very common in British holiday resorts, every Summer, were pretty much phased out altogether, after regular complaints from feminists.

Many feminists then as now, do not share the Christian faith that Mary Whitehouse had but they no doubt have much respect for her. To the great credit of traditional feminists: politicians, lawyers and academics among them – They have helped a great deal in implementing much needed reforms in tackling injustices and sex crimes against women and girls: at home, in schools, workplaces, on public transport, leisure/social settings and everywhere else. It wasn't until the vast scale of Jimmy Savile's crimes were revealed in late 2012, when calls and online messages to women and children's charities, completely skyrocketed, with callers to the helplines being men and women, boys and girls of all ages. The 'swinging sixties' must have been a truly exciting time for teenagers and young adults, with the rise of The Beatles, Bob Dylan, The Who and The Rolling Stones: with fast changing fashions, the advent of television, more electrical appliances and cars being more readily available to everyday people, plus, huge social changes and campaigns, that have shaped much of the world as we know it today. However, the extreme fallout from those fast-changing days with the sexual revolution, the selfish pursuit of hedonism and instant gratification, have been truly catastrophic. Everything must be done to protect women and children from evil predators.

It is widely believed that feminism began as far back as the late 18th century, after Mary Wollstonecraft of London England, wrote 'A vindication of the rights of women', in which she argues for women's education, of which there was very little at the time. Mary passed away, aged thirty-eight. However, her book certainly struck a chord with many women in London, the rest of Britain and further ashore, as the years went by. The first wave of feminism comprised of suffrage: the women's right to vote and stand for parliamentary office, began in Australia and New Zealand in the late 19th century, during the time of British rule, then later on to Britain itself, the United States and Europe. Women in several countries had won the right to vote by the turn of the 20th century, though it still was not permitted in Britain. It was then that the 'Women's Social and Political Union', (WSPU) better known as the suffragette movement, was formed by Emmeline Pankhurst. Militant tactics were later deployed, sometimes involving arson, bombings and with suffragettes regularly chaining themselves to railings, when diplomatic campaigning failed to bring any progress to fruition. Their motto became 'Deeds, not words.' This would later see many arrests and hundreds of suffragettes, sent to prison. Many of the suffragettes began hunger strikes but were often held down and force fed, with nutrients pumped into their stomachs, via the use of tubes. Emily Davison, a hardcore suffragette, ran onto the racecourse of the 1913, Epsom Derby near London and was struck by the Kings horse, being killed in the process. It is widely believed that she tried to dismount the jockey from his horse. Her funeral was attended by thousands. The outbreak of the First World War in 1914, suspended suffragette campaigns but in 1918, women of influence over thirty were permitted to vote. It wasn't until 1928, with the introduction of the Equal Franchise Act, that all women in Britain aged twenty-one and over were given the right to vote, which was later lowered to eighteen years of age. In 1999, Emmeline Pankhurst featured in Time Magazine's '100 most important people of the 20th century' list.

The suffrage movement is now also known as being the 'first wave' of feminism, which history now views, as a just and noble cause. (With the exception of the minority of those suffragettes, who deployed the most extreme tactics.) Up until then, women had no real say on much of their lives. 'Second wave' feminism, which developed from the 1960s to the 1980s, and which started in the United States, then onto Europe and areas of Asia, broadened to a whole other range of issues on family, sexuality, domestic abuse/violence and the 'wage gap.' Much of it was reasonable enough. The movement helped in securing better career options for women and helped to play a vital role in the civil rights movement to implement change for the better, among black Americans and improving opportunities for black women over the decades, who were more likely to be held back, through no fault of their own. A British film, 'Made in Dagenham': a true story, highlighting women, striking at the Ford car plant in the Dagenham area on the east London outskirts in 1968, which gathered news attention in both Britain and beyond, to demand an end to sex discrimination and the right to equal pay. The strike helped to bring forth the UK, Equal Pay Act of 1970. (The Made in Dagenham play has now been made into a theatre musical.)

January 1973 seen the landmark case of 'Roe vs Wade', which started when Norma McCorvey under the pseudonym 'Jane Roe', began a case in her native Texas to seek a termination, after becoming pregnant with her third child. Texas law stated at the time that such a procedure was illegal with very few exceptions, such as an abortion to only be implemented in the event of saving the mother's life. The matter was then taken to the Supreme Court. A 7-2 Supreme Court ruling, fully legalised abortion throughout the United States, which has bitterly divided the American public over the decades, since then. The same can be said for all peoples, the entire world over, where abortion was legalised. The supreme court decided that the right to privacy implied in the 14th amendment, protected abortion as a fundamental right, with individual women and not the government, being able to decide to continue or end a pregnancy. (Much of American, domestic terrorism, since the early seventies has been attributed to attacks on abortion clinics, resulting in the deaths and injuries of numerous Doctors and medical staff, in that time.)

On Friday 24th June 2022, Roe vs Wade was overturned in the case of 'Dobbs vs Jackson, Women's Health Organisation' In 'Dobbs', the Supreme Court reviewed the constitutionality of the Gestational Age Act of

Mississippi, which was a law that banned abortions after fifteen weeks, except for in extreme cases. The Supreme Court voted 6-4 to uphold the Mississippi law, overturning Roe vs Wade (1973) and Planned Parenthood vs Casey, (1992) stating in their conclusion that the Constitution does not protect the right to an abortion. Numerous States, such as Texas, Louisiana, Arkansas and Tennessee, have now either banned abortion outright or will only perform it in extreme circumstances. Some States changed laws with halved restrictions. In California and Colorado, abortion laws are still fully intact. There will no doubt be many legal challenges to come in most or all US States, in the years ahead.

Some cities and States will see (or have seen) higher levels of abortions than others, depending on demographics, poverty levels and other factors. Young, unmarried black mothers under twenty-five from an inner-city neighbourhood are far more likely to seek an abortion than a white, working class woman with three children in a violent relationship. Pro abortion activists will argue that having an abortion will save both the mother and father from financial hardship and the child itself from a life of potential hardship, and possible abuse in the future. Furthermore, this prevents a child from repeating the destructive, generational cycle of his/her own parents in later life. There is also the belief that a developing baby, before ten weeks, is merely a 'blob' and not at the actual 'baby/human' stage at this time. This, despite overwhelming evidence to the contrary: thanks to far more advanced scanning and greater, cutting edge technology, since the turn of the twenty-first century, that shows that the brain, heart, limbs and much of the vital organs have formed by the seventh week alone. Experts estimate, the ten-week developing baby, possesses approximately 90% of the 4,500 body parts, found in adults.

True Christians believe that a baby is human from the moment of conception. And it is for that reason that Christians and hundreds of millions of people of other faiths, rightfully get angry, when simplistic words like 'choose' and 'choice' are used by those who support the need for abortion. (Choice, is what the colour of your next car should be and wondering what to have to eat, while browsing through the menu of an Italian restaurant. For such words to be used in the 'debate' on abortion, is just simply grotesque.)

So many young and older women, from all cultures and walks of life, the entire world over, bitterly regret having had an abortion, after many were falsely assured by professionals and family members alike, that the procedure is not much different to having a tooth or an appendix being removed, with many women and girls being terribly damaged by their decision, (many often coerced into doing so) for the rest of their lives, wondering what their son or daughter would have looked like and what they might have gone on to achieve in adult life.

World famous individuals such as Jack Nicholson, Cher, Steve Jobs, Justin Bieber, Celine Dion and the soccer legend, Cristiano Ronaldo, were close to being aborted when their own mothers were pregnant with them. Each and every abortion is an absolute tragedy. There is a whole array of adoption agencies, with many loving couples upon their registers, whose backgrounds are always, rigorously checked and who are able to offer a child a decent quality of life. Natural parents, depending on their character and lifestyle, are sometimes given the chance to be reunited with their child. If they are in a better situation than they were and there is a good bond with child and parent over the course of time, sometimes, the child can be returned to them.

'Third wave' feminists have no new agenda as such from second wave feminists, though they are more racially inclusive and more militant in their campaigning. Many such women are more likely to dislike men and blame them for their woes, especially if they have been abused by a male relative and/or partner in the past. They are far more likely to have far left beliefs, have support for the transgender community and deeply resent those feminists who do not, such as the Harry Potter author, JK Rowling: who once used to be universally revered as a feminist icon, who overcame poverty and also abuse in her first marriage, to achieve super stardom as one of Britain's most famous authors and becoming a self-made billionaire – And also the Australian feminist, Germaine Greer. These feminists are typically referred to as TERFs: Trans Exclusionary,

Radical Feminists. This, despite the fact that there is nothing 'radical' about their views. JK Rowling, has often borne the brunt of having protestors turn up to events she attends and has even had protestors outside the gates of her Edinburgh home, to protest at her views: a method of protest known as 'doxxing', often displaying banners and with Ms Rowling often requiring police protection. Numerous celebrities, including the Harry Potter actor, Daniel Radcliffe himself, have rebuked and disowned JK Rowling for her views, insisting that trans women are women, who should be given the same status and legal rights as biological women.

What exactly, would Emmeline Pankhurst and her fellow suffragettes of the years gone by, have made of all of what has happened, in the years following the campaigns for suffrage and being given the right to vote? What would they make of the entitled, butch, young women with multi coloured hair and rings through their noses, screaming insults and obscenities at those who merely disagree with their views? The suffragettes were not exactly shrinking violets themselves either, it certainly has to be said, However, for the most part, these women remained dignified and steadfast, while challenging long established and institutional, all male hierarchies and hence, why they gradually won over the support of the general public in their respective nations and helped to implement much needed changes for the better.

Attitudes towards sexual harassment, assault and violence, have changed a great deal for the better, during my own lifetime, since my birth in December 1976. What a celebrity or person of influence could get away with on a regular basis in my earlier years, would now see imprisonment and disgrace. The international, '#MeToo movement' has played a huge role in seeing the likes of Harvey Weinstein and R. Kelly, put behind bars. On a regular level, no woman, nowhere, should have to dread going on public transport and stepping into her workplace. Nor should they have to endure unwanted attention at social events and to be patronised at, to 'take it easy' and 'liven up' by others. More CCTV, now present on public transport and public venues, have thankfully cut down such unwanted attention and harassment by a great deal. Traditional aspects of feminism have helped to make numerous, positive impacts to improve the lives of women and girls for the better. But very sadly, whether by accident or design, many millions of people, the entire world over, blame the more modern aspects of feminism for the break-up of the traditional family unit, which in turn has been responsible for huge levels of social breakdown and disorder, over the years.

Part Two

Rise Of The Manosphere

In the years following Elliott Rodger's, shooting spree, I never really gave the incel movement, MGTOW and pick up artists, that much thought. The BBC had done a documentary on the subject, titled 'Reggie Yates', Extreme UK: Men at war.' This programme, which featured controversial figures, such as Milo Yiannopoulos, who once famously stated that "Feminism is cancer" and one of the most well-known pick up artists (PUAs) and author of often, deeply offensive literature, Daryush Valizadeh: better known in the manosphere movement as 'Roosh V.' The documentary was average at best. With the exception of the Alek Minassian, van attack in Toronto Canada in 2018, the British media gave very little coverage on anything to do with the manosphere movement, during the late 2010s.

During one Saturday evening in early 2021, while on YouTube, I seen an algorithm, displaying a video for a guest speaker who went by the title of 'Coach Greg Adams', who was talking to an audience on a stage about 'The Jezebel Spirit' on a platform hosted by an Orlando Florida based organisation, called '21 Studios.'

I initially thought he was a preacher and watched it. While the subject matter was indeed, about Jezebel: the manipulating and wicked, Baal and Asherah worshipping Queen, as mentioned in the Old Testament book of 1 Kings, the discussion in more depth, was actually a secular one, in order to warn modern men of similar women who may take advantage of them and lead them astray, in the way Jezebel did with the weak, King Ahab.

21 Studios is a manosphere movement founded by the often, deeply controversial, Anthony 'Dream' Johnson, who regularly wears hats that bear the slogan 'Make Women Great Again', and whose numerous, stage events, feature various speakers and figures from across The United States, Canada and several other countries. (The events can be best described as being similar to the well-known, 'TED talks', that have proven to be very popular online, in recent history.) Over the following months, I began to watch even more videos that the 'Coach' had made, sometimes watching up to three hours of content on Saturday evenings, with videos and channels, covering a whole array of various subjects.

Many of the videos were reasonable enough and some were a bit on the edgy side. Coach Greg Adams rarely slips up on using bad language and much of his content on his own YouTube channels are humorous and good natured. It was shortly after discovering his content, that algorithms then led me to come across the often deeply controversial, 'Fresh & Fit' podcast, which is hosted from the dizzy heights of an exclusive, Miami penthouse and hosted by the 'Fresh Prince CEO', Walter Weekes, who emigrated to America from the Caribbean Island of Barbados, and former, Homeland Security Investigations (HSI) special agent, Myron Gaines, (real name, Amrou Fudl) the second generation son of Sudanese immigrants. The Fresh & Fit podcast gained over one million YouTube subscribers, in late 2022.

Most of the guests on the show, usually comprise of seven or more, often scantily clad, young women and sometimes with one or two male guests in the mix. The topics discussed, cover relationships, male and female nature, various opinions and facts. The layout of the studio looks very similar to a typical, VIP section of an exclusive nightclub, along with neon imagery and aesthetics, very similar to what you would find in similar establishments in downtown Miami. The table is set close to huge, sliding, windowed doors and a balcony, offering fantastic views of the city and coastline below. There is a team of technicians, door staff and a producer, (Aaron) just behind the scenes.

The debates can often get very emotional and heated to the point where they can sometimes get ugly and certain guests will be told to leave the podcast. The shows are always recorded live, usually lasting over two hours, and with the most memorable scenes being cut down into clips, which usually get larger amounts of views. Other shows will have less guests, male guests only and no guests at all, with only the hosts in discussion. (Both hosts, each have their own separate, online shows, between them.) Viewers can also give their own opinions on the subjects being discussed, which are known as 'super-chats', and which appear on screen, for a minimal fee. Many guests often donate $50 or more.

While many women often come under fire for their lifestyles and their views on the show, men of all backgrounds, also come under the 'hairdryer' of the hosts, on a regular basis: which also includes celebrities, sports stars and people of influence, for being simps in their relationships and being with women who 'belong to the streets' in their view - Eg: Promiscuous, self-centred, gold digging women who don't seem to genuinely care for the men in their lives. The Hollywood actor and entertainer, Will Smith, came under severe criticism from Fresh & Fit (and not to mention, just about the entire manosphere movement) for slapping the comedian, Chris Rock, at the 2022 Academy Awards, after he made a joke about his wife Jada's, hair thinning, alopecia condition, then cursing at him after sitting back down. This, despite of the fact that Will Smith laughed at the joke in hand at first before seeing Jada's disgusted reaction, straight after. Later on that night, Will Smith won his first ever, Academy Award for best actor in the film, King Richard: playing Richard Williams, the Father of legendary tennis player sisters,

Venus and Serena Williams, who devoted as much of his spare time as possible, making huge sacrifices, going above and beyond and striving tirelessly against the overwhelming odds, to pave the way for his daughters to rise to tennis stardom, to then be able to move the family away from the mean streets of Compton in Los Angeles and for both sisters to become immortalised as being among the greatest sportswomen in history.

Will Smith, they believe, ruined what would and should have been, the greatest night of his life and career. He later apologised to Chris Rock, the Academy Awards and the Williams family for his conduct that evening but many will feel that the damage now done will scar his reputation for good. Many otherwise, good and easy-going men, have had a rush of blood to the head and, in the space of just a few seconds, gone on to inflict violence and badly injure or even kill someone over a mere quip and/or social media message, often in regards to someone they love. Will Smith has been condemned by anti-violence campaigners, for his actions. This, at a time when black on black violence is staggeringly high in numerous, US cities. Will Smith is often mocked as being a 'white knight' and 'super-simp' for his actions and that Jada's true love was in fact, the murdered rapper, Tupac Shakur, whom she dated in earlier times and very possibly, would have went on to marry, had he not been killed in September 1996. (There were many rumours over the years, regarding Will and Jada having an 'open marriage.' Jada has since revealed in

October 2023, that she and Will have actually been separated, though not divorced, since 2016. This would have probably come as no surprise to many people in the wider, film and entertainment industry, along with their most ardent fans.) Bloggers, such as Fresh & Fit believe the relationship of Will and Jada is very typical of many millions of relationships across the world, in that so many couples are in unhappy, institutionalised, stale marriages and relationships. As far as I know, there is no academically held research on this matter, most possibly due to the sensitive nature of the subject at hand.

According to the manosphere, many single and childless, career driven women will regularly sleep with multiple, 'Chad' men and will fall in love with one or two of them, but will inevitably be turned down or dumped by them, that is, if they even manage to form any relationship at all, for someone younger and better looking than them, before they reach thirty years of age. These women will blame men for their woes and do not take accountability for their own, poor lifestyle choices. They will even resent happily married women, including friends and relatives, who enjoy stability and with often happy, well-loved and well-behaved children. As these women approach their late thirties to forties, the more better-looking guys will longer be interested in them. The overwhelming majority of men, will not want to be with someone who has a history of promiscuity and who comes with 'emotional baggage.' And rightly so. The only men who will want to be with them and marry them, will be the simps: who they settle for but who they never truly respect or love. They are usually troubled men who have been single for most of their lives and/or divorced men, aged forty or over. Friendly and easy going but emotionally weak, such men may be able to provide a good home and even financial security. However, for the woman who settles down with him, this will never substitute the fact that she could have, indeed should have, got married in her prime years and settled down with a loving husband that she could be well and truly proud of, along with children of her own.

These women, often without children, are now in a deeply unhappy, often sexless marriage. They will often belittle and berate their husbands on a regular basis. Divorces (and infidelity, often on the woman's behalf) are a common factor, and with the soon to be ex-wife, often being legally able to take half of his savings. There are regular rumours among the manosphere that some women marry simp men, just to get at his savings, though there is no concrete evidence to prove this theory. Any other relationships they may have in later life, inevitably never last long and they often end up as stereotypical, embittered, 'mad cat ladies' for the rest of their lives, with many becoming misandrists: militant, men hating feminists. Coach Greg Adams, often displays a bizarre but somewhat unique chart that he made, called 'The marriage wheel', which describes why so many modern marriages fail among millions of couples, including financially stable couples who tie the knot in their mid-twenties and who even get off to the best start possible, for a whole variety of reasons. The late, Kevin Samuels, a black man, often singled out black, American women for their destructive lifestyles, as they hold by far, the highest rates for single motherhood, literally anywhere on the face of the Earth, and for having the highest rates of abortions with the vast majority of their pregnancies, being the result of consensual sex. The rapper Kanye West, in an interview with Piers Morgan in October 2022, even quoted: "The most dangerous place for a black person in America is inside their mother's stomach." (Those men who impregnate women, regardless of colour and background, and who choose to have little or no role in their children's lives, are deeply despised by the entire spectrum of the movement.)

The controversial comedian, Dave Chappelle, also made a case in point, in which he stated that he was neither for abortion nor against it. However, if a woman can say 'My body, my choice', with the father being legally unable to stop the mother from undergoing the procedure, then by the very same logic, he should also not be made to pay any child support, should she decide to keep the baby and therefore be able to say: 'My money, my choice.' Many men, mostly good and loving fathers, some of whom are denied access to their children, have been financially ruined, having to pay extortionate amounts in child support payments via the family court system and with many being unable to pay the costs, being locked up behind bars, in the process. Kevin Samuels was often quick to remind these women that the poverty they may face, thus being the main factor for why they terminate their pregnancies, is nowhere near as bad as the poverty faced by hundreds of millions of women and girls in Africa and much of Asia. His sentiments are universally echoed by other black manosphere bloggers, who hold Kevin Samuels in the highest regard and who also pour scorn on millions of black men for their own destructive lifestyles and excuses.

At this time, there are around seventy or so, very well-known figures in the mainstream, manosphere movement. Other notable figures include Rollo Tomassi, Donovan Sharpe, Richard Cooper, Justin Waller, and Richard Grannon. There are also several hundred more 'wannabe' figures, hoping to climb up through the ranks, with many more yet to come. Many bloggers and their followers, find inspiration from stoicism and will often quote many of the most famous philosophers in history such as Aristotle, Plato, Seneca, Confucius and Marcus Aurelius. On their webpages and social media accounts, they will often have imagery of ancient, Greek architecture, culture, statues of philosophers, warriors and images of ancient Greek and Spartan weaponry and armour. Many also look up to leading, literary and modern figures, such as Jordan B. Peterson, Patrick Bet-David, Joe Rogan, Douglas Murray and Peter Hitchens.

By far, the best-known figure in the current, manosphere movement is Andrew Tate – The son of the late, former, world chess champion, Emory Tate. Born in Chicago in December 1986, his family moved to Luton England when he was six years old, becoming a child, chess prodigy himself, before becoming a world champion kickboxer. He became more well known to the British public while being a contestant in the 2016 edition of 'Big Brother', then later on, along with his brother Tristan, making his name and acquiring, global fame on YouTube and other, social media outlets. His many, social media videos and short clips have often seen Andrew Tate, his brother Tristan and their close associates, driving high performance, sports cars, enjoying glasses of champagne, while flying across to other countries in private jets and enjoying the nightlife in some of the most glitzy and glamorous venues that are to be found in the greatest cities on Earth. The huge appeal, that this has on millions of young minds is indeed, very understandable. His views and opinions have truly angered many feminists and also, in very recent times, the British, mainstream media, who write about him on a regular basis: the majority of which is usually negative, although this does not bother him or his legions of fans. Andrew Tate is also friends with Luton's other well-known resident, Stephen Yaxley-Lennon, who is better known to the world by his alias – Tommy Robinson: the co-founder of the English Defence League and constant thorn in the side of the British authorities. Andrew Tate's brother, Tristan, is also a well-known figure within the manosphere movement and they both currently reside in Bucharest Romania. Both brothers are always keen to tell the world that, despite the fact that Romania and the former Eastern Bloc nations are poorer in comparison to the United States and western Europe, marriages there are far stronger and last longer on average, with crime rates lower and with the streets being generally safer at night.

This, they believe, is because Christianity is far more prevalent and untainted within their societies. Their governments, police, schools and places of higher education, have not been corrupted by woke ideals and feminist doctrines. Long established, Islamic communities, are also very common in much of the Balkans region of Europe. Romania, Hungary, Poland, Czech Republic and Slovakia, are among the nations which have endured two different occupations during the twentieth Century: first from Nazi Germany and then later on by the Soviet Union during the Cold War. It is hardly surprising then, that these nations and their peoples, have a very proud and strong sense of identity and who do not take kindly to orders coming to them from anywhere else. These aforementioned nations have had a fairly tense relationship with the European Union, in which they all joined in May 2004, especially in regards to their strong reluctance to accept refugees and migrants escaping war, hardship and conflict from Syria, Iraq and elsewhere. The European Union demanded for these nations to accept a certain, fixed quota of migrants and refugees, which they refused to accept. This was very evident when Germany opened their borders to genuine, Syrian refugees for a time, during the height of the ongoing, civil war there in 2015. The majority of the Eastern Bloc nations, built razor wire fences along their borders, to deter migrants and refugees from entering and settling within their respective nations and also making the journey of those trying to make their way to Germany from Greece, the first European country the huge majority entered, upon arrival to Europe, even harder, much to the anger of the then German Chancellor, Angela Merkel and the European Union leaders in Brussels. The billionaire globalist, George Soros, is deeply despised by many of his fellow Hungarians. Patriotism and identity make for a strong part of the DNA of such nations. (The Polish day of independence on November 11th, is always celebrated in the capital Warsaw, with intense fervour.)

It is among these very reasons, that the Tate brothers decided to move and operate from Bucharest, the capital city of Romania. It is also from their premises, where the Tate brothers run their 'War Room' which is a tight knit group of men who travel from all over the world and, for a substantial fee, learn how to be, in their words, among the very best and successful of men in all areas of life, regarding relationships, finance, fitness, self-confidence and much more. (From Romania, they also run their online courses, such as the: 'Hustlers University' and 'The Real World.') In late December 2022, the Tate brothers were arrested, along with two young women on supposed, human trafficking, rape and organised crime charges. They were released several months later, without charge, though proceedings are still ongoing, at this current time.

Andrew Tate appeared as a guest on the Fresh & Fit show back in 2022, with the discussion during one particular moment, being about women concentrating on their careers and putting marriage and starting a family on the backburner. Several, young women on that particular show, vowed to never become mothers in order to focus on their careers and to enjoy their time socialising, partying and travelling the world with friends. One of the young ladies quoted that her career would be her 'baby', so to speak. Andrew Tate then gave his no holds barred reaction to what they said, which has since been regarded as one of the most memorable moments in the podcast's history, so far. I have shortened it, tweaked it slightly and of course, removed the expletives:

"A life without children is vapious, and its inane and its pointless. And you may sit here and think that your career matters, but the truth is that your job will fire you on a whim and will not care about you. And when you're fifty-two, and you're past it, with no grandchildren, in a house by yourself, and all your friends have grandchildren, this beautiful life, and

you're sitting there by yourself, you think the fact that you can afford a few extra, Gucci bags, is going to genuinely make you feel happy? I was at my grandmothers, 93rd birthday. My grandmother had nine children: there was my father and eight more. They all had a bunch of kids, blah, blah, blah. I stood there and looked at my 93-year-old grandmother and there was a room – A whole room full of maybe seventy people – That came from that one woman! Isn't that remarkable, that nobody cared about her career, nobody asked what job she did, nobody asked how many times she went to the club, nobody asked if she ever had time to go to festivals, no! You had seventy, sentient beings, including myself, full of life from one woman who dedicated herself to being a mother and a good wife. That is beautiful! And if you sit here and genuinely think that you're going to work your way through your fertile years and by the age of fifty-four, you're not going to be suicidal, alone with a cat, then you're wrong…..The happiest women on Earth have children and a man who is paying the bills and are mothers, the happiest people on Earth. I guarantee it. Ask your own mother - Do you regret having me? She is going to say of course not! You're the best thing that ever happened to me. So, now you're going to sit here and end your own bloodline? It's absolutely insulting to your entire bloodline! Everything, everyone above you has ever done and struggled for. All the times your grandparents went to work when they didn't feel like it, just for you to exist, for you to say no, me, my passions, my dreams and my terrible drawings and my Instagram page is more important than ever having children. You're selfish! You should all have kids."

Both, the hosts and guests on the show, were taken aback by what he had said and it certainly got more and more people talking about him. Andrew Tate's, views and opinions are considered to be among the most controversial in all of the mainstream, manosphere movement. One of one most well-known opinions, being that women should 'bear responsibility' if the victim of a sex attack at night, while drinking too much and wearing too little, and that 'depression is not real.' Some of the views among the manosphere bloggers vary on different subjects. Hardly surprising then, that some bloggers do not think highly of other, rival figures within the movement and the way their rivals may present themselves, and their shows. There are however, some things that the manosphere, feminists and Christians can all agree on: Alcoholism, drugs, pornography and gambling are all destructive to men and women alike and which often cause huge distress to the loved ones of addicts. These are common subjects, regularly discussed in the manosphere. Former addicts within the movement, to their credit, explain how horrendous their struggles were and how they overcome their addictions. (The 'Onlyfans' webpage and similar, are very deeply despised by the manosphere, as are those who subscribe to any members on the platform, and rightly so, as is obesity, laziness and excessive computer game and social media usage, among both sexes.)

There are numerous, commonly held views and beliefs, among just about the entire manosphere movement, including PUA's, incels and the MGTOW adherents, of which feminists and even Christians, may find deeply offensive. The manosphere often go by the motto of putting 'facts over feelings' and 'reals over feels' in their often, divisive discussions.

TOPICS, VIEWS AND FACTS

In the subchapter, we will see some highly, emotionally charged, viewpoints and opinions with occasional, government backed facts, thrown in, that will shock and possibly even offend. The social media platforms of well known, manosphere bloggers, their discussions and topics shown online, the likes of which, often gain views in the hundreds of thousands, sometimes millions, which have a strange magnetism to their many viewers, inasmuch the same way, controversial talk shows like 'The Jerry Springer Show' and its British equivalent, 'The Jeremy Kyle Show' had done so, during their time on air. Both shows, regularly came under severe criticism from much of the mainstream media, politicians and the general public alike, over those years but always had sizeable viewing figures before they were eventually taken off the airwaves. The same applies to those comedians and documentary makers (most notably, from UK's, Channel 4) who are forever trying to push boundaries, with often tasteless and sexually themed content.

Among frequently discussed topics are the following:

'The Matrix.'

Andrew Tate, often quotes 'The Matrix' as being a global conspiracy like system (also in reference to the sci-fi movie franchise of the same name) that wants to keep the overwhelming majority of men the entire world over, fat, broke, weak and effeminate, in order that they will be enslaved and controlled more easily by the sinister, powers that be and to prevent them from rising up against this tyrannical, globalist, militant feminist and uber woke, led regime. This system wants to turn strong and confident 'Alpha' males into passive and subservient, 'Beta' males. Mr Tate feels it is his mission, spurred on even more now by his Islamic faith, to help men 'conquer the slave mindset' brought on by The Matrix, which will try to stop anyone who diligently promotes masculinity and traditional values. As he was led away by Police from his home in Bucharest Romania in December 2022 on suspicion of rape and human trafficking activities, along with his brother Tristan and two females, he even quoted to reporters who were present: "The Matrix has attacked me." Many believe these are false allegations and these powers will stop at nothing to destroy him and those like him.

Regular, negative portrayal of men.

In much of the regular, entertainment industry and television commercials, men are often portrayed as hopelessly clumsy, incompetent, bumbling and often weak, in as much the same way Homer Simpson is portrayed, in 'The Simpsons', cartoon franchise. Male characters in the 'Friends' sitcom series were often portrayed as being overly emotional and effeminate. Over the years, I have to admit that I have lost count of ridiculous scenes where men have found themselves being unable to attach a nappy to their baby son or daughter, of men cooking a romantic dinner, only for it to come out all charred black, the burnt meal, bellowing out smoke and setting the fire alarm off and with men awaiting their laundry in a washing machine, for it to then suddenly, burst open and leave the kitchen covered in bubbles. In years gone by, we all laughed at shows like 'The Three Stooges' and films like 'Three Men and A Baby', in which men accidentally made total fools of themselves. We laughed because the scrapes they got into were so ridiculously absurd. Now, we are shown such scenes on an almost, daily basis, especially on television commercials. If there were near, daily scenes in equal measure on adverts and comedies, of women falling off stepladders and bicycles, such shows would be vilified by feminists and the media alike. The 2023 Barbie movie, even has the slogan: 'She's everything. He's just Ken.' (Imagine the furore, if this was said the other way around.)

The 'sexual market place.'

It is widely regarded that a woman is at her prime, during her most fertile years, aged eighteen to twenty-five years of age. Her looks and figure are her main 'currency', so to speak, hence the reason why the beauty, make-up and cosmetics industry is a multi-billion industry that pretty much never suffers, not even during the toughest of economic times. The good looks of a young lady can even help someone working in a fast food restaurant or supermarket, get further ahead than an Oxbridge graduate, her own age, if she happens to be spotted by a talent scout, working for a reputable, beauty/cosmetics firm, magazine or similar. This will open many doors for her, leading to even greater opportunities and she could very well end up marrying an influential man in music or sports. And, although a great deal of women will remain very attractive for a good while, they will all eventually, 'hit the wall', as manosphere bloggers often describe it, usually by the age of thirty-five to forty-five, when their fertile years are just about over and looks slowly begin to decline, even more so, later on, during the onset of the menopause. Myron Gaines of Fresh and Fit fame, has often quoted to his female guests that 'men age like wine, women age like milk', much to their fury.

Women are strongly encouraged to start a family first, rather than starting a career, or to put their career on hold for several years and return to their job, part time. As mentioned earlier, full on, career women who end up childless are never as happy as those who have married and had children. Entertainment shows, such as 'Sex and the City', are often slammed by the manosphere for a deeply false portrayal of the 'strong, independent woman', living an equally, happy and fulfilling life, as their married counterparts. (I have never watched one episode of Sex and the City and never intend to. The title itself is more than enough to put me off it.)

Accountability of women.

This subject is of course, a very emotive one and one that goes back to the beginning of the sexual revolution, when more revealing clothing among women, out and about, started to become the norm. While the mainstream manosphere, strongly condemns anyone who commits sexual assault and rape, an intoxicated, flirty woman, wearing revealing clothing in a run-down bar, nightclub or event, frequented by less than savoury people, is putting herself at terrible risk. One of the most talked about films of the late 1980s was 'The Accused', starring Jodie Foster, and which was loosely based on a true story of a gang rape victim in Massachusetts USA, back in 1983. This often, hard to watch film, in which Foster's character, Sarah Tobias, also faces intimidation by her attackers, after her ordeal and later on, faces intense cross examination by their lawyer in court, in regards to what she was wearing, how much she had to drink and also on her own behaviour, during that dreadful night, continues to divide opinion to this very day.

Feminists will strongly argue that a woman should be able to wear as little as she wishes, at any time of night, in her leisure hours and that 'patriarchal' men are trying to 'control' women, their bodies and their lives. On the contrary, good men and decent, loving fathers of teenage girls in particular are in fact, trying to keep their daughters safe. When a Father barks at his daughter: "You're not going out in that!" – He does so out of love and to keep her safe. It is not because he is being a controlling bully, trying to spoil her good time. By the time that said, teenager in question is a young lady, when she does go out at night, she will dress and act responsibly, she will stay in a tight knit, group of sensible and caring friends and will certainly not return to the home of any man, especially one that she happened to have met in the club that night. If she meets a man she likes and he is of good character, they will exchange phone numbers. Those women who do sleep with men they have only met, just hours before, more often than not, have had no proper father figure or male role models in their lives to help guide them through life. They are more prone to sexually transmitted infections and unwanted pregnancies. (Many of which will sadly be aborted.) Women who make poor lifestyle choices are very rarely held accountable for their poor decisions in the same way that men are. It is often seen by much of mainstream society to be 'judgemental' and 'cruel' to speak and rebuke them over such matters.

> In like manner also, that women adorn
> themselves in modest apparel, with
> shamefacedness and sobriety; not with
> broided hair, or gold, or pearls, or costly
> array. (1 Timothy 2:9 KJV.)

Just like these loving fathers, our loving God, knows too well, the hearts of evil men and he too, wants to keep all women and girls safe. Anyone who leaves a window slightly open in their home while away on holiday, certainly does not deserve to be burgled. But, very sadly, that is the world in which we live in. And you just can't sugar coat it. The overwhelming majority of attacks, which are of a sexual nature, are completely avoidable if a young lady makes sensible decisions in regards to her lifestyle choices, the calibre of friends she has within her inner circle and the willingness to be able to steer clear of certain, toxic places and toxic people, regardless of any peer pressures.

The 'Body Positivity' movement.

This has been a growing movement, which started around the late 2000s to early 2010s, and encourages women to feel comfortable with whatever weight and size that they may happen to be. The morbidly obese 'plus size' model, Tess Holliday, appeared on the cover of the UK edition of the Cosmopolitan magazine in October 2018. Not surprisingly, the magazine faced a huge backlash and the movement has come under severe criticism: not just from the manosphere, but also from a fair percentage of society, comprising of both sexes. While it is a cause for concern when some young women and girls, literally starve themselves to become thin and end up becoming anorexic in the process, while trying to look like the models they see online, strutting the catwalks of Paris and Milan, on the opposite side of the scale, the rates of obesity throughout the United States, Canada, much of Europe and beyond, continue to rise, leading to diabetes, heart disease and a whole array of problems and early deaths while also draining billions from the economies of many nations, year in, year out.

Mainstream, manosphere bloggers, strongly urge their followers to refrain from dating obese women at all costs. (Black men are often singled out and given the 'hairdryer' treatment by black manosphere bloggers for this subject matter on a regular basis.) Men who date obese women and who marry them, are viewed as simps. Women with numerous tattoos and/or piercings are not seen in a positive light by the manosphere, either. Fans of manosphere bloggers are regularly told that you have to judge a book by its cover when it comes to women. Obesity, tattoos, excessive piercings (especially nose rings) and even clothing and forms of make-up are 'red flags' to stay away from. Coach Greg Adams often quotes that some women have 'more red flags than a Chinese parade', so to speak. Myron Gaines of Fresh & Fit fame, has often pointed out that if a body positivity movement for men were to arise, it would become the subject of absolute ridicule. It is for this reason they strongly believe, that an obese man is usually far more determined than an obese woman, to try and lose weight. And is therefore, usually more successful in doing so.

Dating single mothers:

Just about the entire spectrum of the manosphere movement, strongly urge their followers to avoid forging relationships with single mothers at all costs. This is one that I personally find very hard to agree with, due to the fact that my own mother was a single mother with my brother Dave, when she and my Father first met in a local, public house, where she done part time bar work, back in 1975. I put my feelings aside and studied the views of others on this matter, regardless. Much of it was very interesting. My parents are still together after forty-eight years at this time, although it would appear that the longevity of their relationship, seems to be the extreme exception and certainly not the norm. Relationships and marriages with single mothers in this current age, never tend to last beyond seven years on average. A man may end up marrying a single mother, invest huge amounts of his own time, effort and money towards a child or children that are not biologically his own, to then, possibly, end up becoming divorced and then have no legal access to his now, former stepchildren, whatsoever. A man will have responsibility but no authority. (A man with both natural children and stepchildren brings 'much trouble' upon himself, according to mainstream, manosphere bloggers.) Even if a divorced man has no legal access to his own, biological children, during their childhood age, his children, once they reach adult age, provided their father was not violent or abusive, are far more likely to forge a relationship with him, than the adult, former stepchildren that a man did once have. This is also a very emotive subject, as there are indeed, many, many lovely single mothers out there, which cannot be denied. It does indeed anger me, when some bloggers suggest, that single mothers are merely looking for a 'meal ticket' and that they should only be 'used' by men for what certain bloggers crudely describe, as being 'for recreational purposes only.'

Well-meaning men who fall in love with single mothers and who have genuine intentions of trying to enrich their children's lives, are viewed as being 'white knights' and 'super simps.' They are furthermore, the subject of severe criticism and ridicule by much of the manosphere. Viewing many hours of videos and blogs on just this one subject alone, I personally, would strongly encourage any man to think very long and hard before potentially starting any relationship with any single mother, out there. Her lifestyle, the behaviour of her children and her treatment of them, her family, the calibre of her circle of friends and how she keeps her home. If any red flags are evident, then it is indeed, best to stay away.

Women in the workplace.

As already mentioned, women are often falsely told by much of society and the Hollywood industry, that staying single, focusing on your career and going out on 'dates', which is a euphemism for having casual sex with different men, every now and then, is equally as fulfilling as being married with children. Motherhood is naturally hardwired into girls from their earliest years, hence the reason why girls play with baby dolls, toy prams and buggies, from the moment that they are able to walk. Motherhood is a gift from God. Not every woman, who wishes to have children, can have them, for a variety of reasons. The manosphere does not insist that women never work again after having children but that looking after children must always take precedence. Hence, never again, working over thirty hours a week from then on. (With the exception being that of medical, emergency services and high-ranking professions.) Full time motherhood should always be considered, if it is at all possible. I was lucky enough in my earlier years, to have never been a 'latchkey kid' upon returning home from school. Mum was always present when I came home, usually preparing dinner. Children, who returned to an empty home until after 6pm, due to the fact that both parents were working and who had to make their own dinner, are more likely to struggle at school and have a greater likelihood of mental health problems in later, adult life. Some women are fortunate enough to create an ideal work and family life balance, without facing burnout and marital problems but this is often, very hard to achieve. The manosphere believe the 'gender pay gap' argument is deeply flawed for numerous reasons as in just about every, western nation, it is illegal to pay women less for the exact same job as a man. Women will need maternity leave, usually while in the second trimester of pregnancy, and usually for months after her giving birth. Women are far more likely to be working part time hours and in less skilled jobs, such as retail and care work. Most of the best paid careers and trades have an overwhelmingly, male workforce, due to the fact that they are more physically demanding and/or involve large amounts of time away from home, and with some being dangerous. Construction, trucking, shipping, oil rigging, mining, farming, aviation, plumbing, mechanics, surgery and the military. Numerous podcasts are quick to point out that women are bigger consumers than men and are far more likely to rack up debts than men, especially if they are single. Therefore, they are more prone to mental health struggles than men, in regards to money matters.

Other: Views on Christianity and other faiths.

Both Christianity and Islam are generally held in high regard by the manosphere, even among their non-believers. The traditional, family unit is often much stronger in Muslim majority nations, as is a strong work ethic and community spirit. Judaism does get mentioned, here and there but other faiths rarely get mentioned. (Many feminists often have a tendency towards Buddhism and new age movements, the latter of which, is often the subject of ridicule by the movement.) Many within the manosphere will agree that Christians from (or originally from) The Caribbean, Central/South America, Sub-Saharan Africa and South East Asia, are typically among the most devoted and passionate of believers in the world today. Any churches that kowtow to LGBT and 'woke' doctrines are very deeply despised by the movement. Many African and Asian Christians, whose forefathers were taught the gospel by British and European missionaries, are now spreading the gospel to British and European people. This is something that would be completely unimaginable in days gone by. It is hardly surprising then, that The Redeemed Christian Church of God, (RCCG) which was founded in Nigeria back in 1952, has not only gone from strength to strength throughout Africa, the church has spread across the whole world and now has over seven hundred churches active, across the UK. Some can be found in predominately white towns, like my own and with many more white people now beginning to attend the services, as they feel that the churches they were attending, have lost their way. The Redeemed Christian Church of God, do much fantastic work and do much to help the most vulnerable in our society, via a whole variety of ways.

Those Christians within the movement, while encouraging good spiritual, marital and financial advice, often quote, that it is wise and the right thing to do, for a man to know and to serve God, first and foremost, marry and settle down, rather than for a man to selfishly and sinfully, devote his life in the hedonistic pursuit of greed, while acquiring wealth and women. And rightly so.

> For what shall it profit a man, if he shall gain the whole world, and lose his own soul? (Mark 8:36 KJV)

Andrew Tate has been quick to point out that many traditional, Christian nations are slowly beginning to fall apart. He often quotes that many within these nations, from political leaders to everyday people have now abandoned God. And God will likewise, abandon them.

Politics:

It is hardly surprising, that just about the entire manosphere movement is right leaning, regardless of the ethnicity, background and nationality of the bloggers. Uber left, leaning nations and US States, often come under ferocious criticism, with the American west coast states of California, Oregon and Washington State, often under the spotlight for their uber liberal laws, that have allowed for degeneracy and wide scale disorder to flourish in some parts. Many within the movement look up to figures such as Donald Trump, Nigel Farage and the current, Hungarian Prime Minister, Viktor

Orban, who all have very tough stances on immigration and crime. There is near universal support among the movement, to build a wall and more barriers along the US/Mexico border and for far more security and razor wire fencing on the borders within continental Europe, along with tougher, sea border controls in both the Mediterranean Sea and the English Channel. Many strongly believe that feminism has blighted politics, helping to pass many of the problematic and uber liberal laws that also, continually demonise men, with more controversial 'hate' laws and with the belief that more female politicians, councillors and interns are more likely to become emotional, rather than rational on all kinds of subjects, and that they are more likely to buckle under pressure, due to their hormones. Many within the manosphere movement have little or no respect for the majority of politicians, senators and councillors within their respective nations, who they feel are only interested in getting rich and who do not care for the everyday people and the country they claim to serve.

Facts and statistics:

The following information is compiled from academic research, that make for sobering reading. These statistics are featured in the Coach Greg Adams book, 'DeEvolution: Feminism's Reverse Engineering of American Women.' Some of these highlights were featured on a large screen at a 21 Convention meeting in Orlando Florida, to the title of:

Strong, Independent women?

60+ million abortions, since 1973.
50% of women are single.
25% of women take mental health medication.
45% of American children are born to unwed mothers.
67% of marriages end in divorce.
80% of divorces are initiated by women.
93% of alimony (child support) paid from men to women.
83% of women receive primary custody of children.
72% of the inmates in State prison were raised by single mothers.

Featured stats within the book also include…..
68% of the US, student loan debt, belongs to women.
66% of women carry, credit card debt.
45% of women aged 25-44 work full time and 85% of them live from paycheck to paycheck.
Women are responsible for 73% of consumer spending in the US.

There is no hiding from the fact, that much of the internal problems faced by the United States and the Western world, combined with the ever increasing levels of violence, drug abuse, sex crimes, debt and despair, to name but a few can indeed, be attributed to the breakdown of the traditional, family unit, the continuous absence of Christian teachings and values and of thoroughly toxic, uber-left, woke teachings, poisoning our institutions, workplaces and our very way of life.

Coach Greg Adams also points out, academically researched statistics, that children of single, unwed mothers without a father or decent, male role model in their lives, are very prone to developing behavioural problems and more likely to struggle at school, become trapped in a cycle of poverty, become more likely to be abused physically and sexually, often by a later partner of his/her mother. They are more likely to develop obesity, diabetes and an array of physical and mental health struggles. There is also the widely and bitterly disputed belief that, from their youngest years, many black, American girls are actively encouraged by their mothers, sisters and female relatives, to get themselves pregnant from the moment they reach adulthood, regardless of whether or not the father is likely to stay around to marry and/or provide for the mother and be there for his child. And of course, children of single mothers are far more likely to engage in drug abuse, alcoholism, crime and end up in the prison system at some stage of their lives. Having a child outside of wedlock, used to be deeply frowned upon in western nations, prior to the sexual revolution. Indeed, it still is in many parts of the world, most notably, in Muslim majority nations. However, single parenthood in some cities, is almost the norm, especially in the inner cities and communities in and around Atlanta, Dallas, New York, Chicago and Los Angeles, to new but a few. In some of these areas within such cities, single mothers outnumber their married counterparts by a great deal.

The most militant of feminists, often tend to get very emotional on such subjects and insist that deeply ingrained, systemic racism, stretching back many years to the era of slavery is to blame for such setbacks among African Americans. The same applies to black and other minority groups in Canada, the United Kingdom, France and South Africa. However, even those in the 'black manosphere' movement, insist that black men and women have no one else to blame but themselves for their own pitfalls and setbacks. Myron Gaines of the Fresh & Fit podcasts, has ranted on numerous occasions, that if Chinese, Korean, Mexican and African people can arrive on American soil, many of whom, often with little money and basic grasp of the English language to begin with, can work hard, open businesses, have solid marriages and are able to fund their children's, college fees, then why on earth can millions of born and bred, black Americans, not do the same?

Myron has spoken on his show that his Sudanese, immigrant father, worked long hours as a taxi driver in New York City, during the 1980s, when crime rates were very high. His father often endured terrible beatings on numerous occasions from drug fuelled passengers and who would start his shift, often with fresh bruises, knowing each time that he may not return home, as killings among taxi drivers increased, during this time. Despite the risks, he still worked as a cabbie for years. During Myron's time as a Homeland Security Investigations agent, he and his team came across a truly horrendous sight of an abandoned, truck trailer full of deceased, Central American and Mexican men, women and children, who died from the searing heat, near San Antonio, Texas. The outside temperature was past 100 Fahrenheit, that day. These poor souls were hoping to make better lives for themselves.

Although most of the guests on the Fresh & Fit podcast are women, most of the people they speak to on the 'phone in' episodes are men. Myron often gets angry at black men who call in and who say that it is not possible for them to progress in life because of their circumstances. While racism and discrimination does sadly exist and must be tackled, the 'black manosphere' firmly believes that the majority of the problems among black communities can be fixed from within via the 'tough love' approach, telling them to stop being in denial of the toxic lifestyles and mindsets that are continually being passed down through the generations and be prepared to face very uncomfortable facts and look to solutions in helping to tackle these grave problems. In both the United Kingdom and the Republic of Ireland, there are ever increasing rates of unwed, mainly single white mothers. (Something unimaginable in pre-1960s time.) This also creates similar issues to those mentioned earlier. It is now widely believed, not just by the manosphere but by millions of people, that there is a hardcore of militant feminists, waging a 'war on men' and 'war on the family', with the grossly perverted view that they are actually trying to 'liberate' women from the so-called patriarchy and are 'empowering' them. Why be 'chained' to a kitchen sink with a crying baby, that has soiled another fresh nappy in the space of two hours, and a husband with continual, bad habits, such as leaving the bathroom and bedroom in a mess, when you can have a full time career, not be woken up by crying at 3am, make all of your own plans, each and every day and travel the world more often, during your prime years to visit the wonders of the world, such as the Grand Canyon and go scuba diving along the Great Barrier Reef, along the north east coast of Australia. Total freedom and bliss.

The world is your oyster, Queen!
Because you're worth it.
Be the inspiration.
Shine bright like a diamond.
Reach for the stars.

All of these are feelgood but ultimately, fruitless slogans in the long run. While these 'free spirit' women may indeed, enjoy a much better quality of life for a certain period of time, the tables will eventually turn around once the married and unmarried woman, reach their mid to late thirties, as mentioned earlier. Yes, crying babies and sleep deprivation are not pleasant experiences, but thankfully, those babies do eventually grow up. Even the best of husbands will be annoying and irritating to their wives, every once in a while, (and vice versa) but that is just part and parcel of everyday life. The idea of marriage, may feel like a daunting prospect to many in this current age. Is it even worth it nowadays? This is a question that both young men and women will continually ask themselves, and rightly so. They will ask that question even more, if the marriage of their own parents was troubled and volatile or were raised in a single parent household. Separation and divorce are incredibly tough and damaging for many, especially if children are involved within the marriage. Divorce rates continue to rise, year on year. A Christ centred, loving marriage is far more likely to stand the test of a couple's lifetime, through the many trials and tribulations, than that of unbelieving couples. Examples of this can be found, the entire world over. Statistically, men and women in strong, Christian marriages tend to live happier, healthier and more productive lives than those who willingly choose to stay single.

WHEN HYPERGAMY BECOMES A CURSE

Throughout the course of human history, up until the mid-twentieth century, the overwhelming majority of men and women, the entire world over, would generally marry someone of a similar, socio-economic background, within a ten-mile radius of where they lived and usually before twenty-six years of age. With the advent of railways in the late nineteenth century, followed later on by the rise of automobiles in the subsequent decades after, greater opportunities lay ahead for families and budding singletons from smaller towns and more rural backgrounds to head to growing, bigger cities for work and to improve prospects to a level that they probably would not have been able to achieve in their town/region of origin. (Numerous, villages in Scotland, were abandoned by their residents altogether in the early to mid-twentieth century, thus moving to Glasgow, Edinburgh or further south into England to seek better opportunities. The legendary, Liverpool FC soccer manager, Bill Shankly, grew up in the former, mining village of Glenbuck in Ayrshire in west Scotland, which has long since been abandoned.)

The advent of passenger aircraft, being more widely available to the general public, since the 1960s, brought with it, even more greater opportunities and prospects, with more marriages of couples from different nationalities and ethnicities. The twentieth century has seen more radical changes than at any other time in history. Marriage rates in some western nations however, with the exception of some ethnic communities, have now rapidly declined to very low levels, since the early to mid-2010s. This, despite the fact that young men and women in general, now have a far better, quality of life than previous generations fared, in terms of more enriching food and safer water, better and safer, living and working conditions, plus with far greater access to improved healthcare. In my home county of Wiltshire in southern England and also many counties throughout Britain and Ireland, it is very common to see cottages with front, back and interior doors being less than six foot high. A typical Englishman in pre-1920s times would probably be around 5'6" tall on average and would be considered lucky if he lived beyond fifty-five years of age. (This, at the time when the Sun never set on the British Empire, being that it was so vast and covered a great deal of the globe at the time of its zenith.)

Hypergamy, as described in Wikipedia, is a term used in social science for the practice of a person marrying a spouse of higher caste or social status than themselves. It is mostly practised by women and colloquially referred to as 'marrying up.'

In more poorer countries, many fathers will do their utmost to send their daughters to more urban areas to improve her life, her marriage prospects and for her to hopefully improve the life of her family back home by eventually sending money back to them. This practice is common in more rural regions of India and China. As long as there is genuine love on both sides, there is nothing wrong with marrying up in this regard. However, since the rise of social media and Instagram in particular, many attractive, young ladies can literally set up an account, upload less than twenty pictures, gain over three thousand followers and be inundated with hundreds of likes, emojis and gushing comments in the space of just five to seven days. Young ladies from the hard up, South Wales Valleys may get messages from men in London and Manchester, offering dinner and romance. Young, attractive ladies from small towns in Nebraska and Kansas, may be offered the same by men in New York, Chicago and Los Angeles. It must no doubt, be an exciting prospect for these ladies to leave behind the drudgery of their humble surroundings for the bright lights of the big cities to meet handsome and prosperous men.

There is a fast growing and popular belief, that 80% of women under thirty are vying for the attention of the top 20% of the most good looking and wealthiest of high value men, with the long-term pursuit of hopefully marrying such a high value man. And that there are a hardcore among that number of women, trying their absolute utmost to win over the attention of the top 1% of men: the millionaires and playboys, living jet setting lifestyles that very few of us 'mere mortals' can even begin to imagine.

However, in most cases, many of these high value men are often in contact with many more women. It is strongly believed throughout the manosphere, that many women will already be fully aware of this and will even be prepared to be cheated on, every so often, provided that she acquires the lifestyle she ultimately wants. Very few such women will ever get married to such a man anyway, as he will more than likely finish with her for someone younger by the time she reaches twenty-eight years of age. (The Hollywood actor, Leonardo DiCaprio, is very well known for doing this.) Nevertheless, millions of women are chasing a Disney style dream that very, very few, will ever go on to achieve, that also involves no infidelity and a happy ever after. Ladies need to realise this very uncomfortable truth: winning over a millionaire who is over six feet tall, earning a six figure (or more) salary, who is super muscular, exudes super confidence, with a social media following in the tens of thousands, who wishes to settle down and start a family, while being constantly loyal and loving throughout, is probably as rare as a national lottery win! Possibly even more rare than that.

It seems that too many, celebrity obsessed women are in denial about these facts. For most ladies with large, social media followings, any dates they may have with any influential men, will almost certainly be very short lived, leading to bitter jealousy and rage, once these men, almost inevitably, turn their attention to someone else. Very sadly, a fraction of such women will go down the very slippery slope of setting up an 'OnlyFans' account or similar, and/or become involved in the so-called, adult entertainment industry. Hundreds, possibly thousands of such women have since, destroyed promising careers and their own reputations for the lure of cheap fame and easy money. Both men and women who have or have had, been involved in the adult industry, very sadly, suffer higher rates of mental health struggles, drug abuse and suicides than among the general population. OnlyFans is often referred to as 'lonely fans' by the manosphere – And with good reason. No decent, respectable man will ever want to forge a relationship with a woman who has or had, any involvement with OnlyFans or similar. Once these women pass thirty, they are destined for bitter loneliness and/or continuous, unhappy relationships with simps.

Many women, it is believed, are attracted to the 'bad boys' that can be found in many towns and just about every city, in the western world. This, despite the fact, that the chances of taming and marrying such a man are extremely slim, regardless of how attractive she may be. From the Manchester United soccer icon, George Best, who famously quoted "I spent a lot of money on booze, birds and fast cars. The rest, I just squandered" – to Russell Brand to the boxing legend, Mike Tyson: many women will flock to these uniquely talented but often troubled and unpredictable men, and those similar to them, in their droves. Millions of women are also attracted to famous rap stars and the many thousands of wannabes: the 'Z-list' DJ's, singers and rappers in nightclubs, the world over. This, despite the fact that many of their lyrics in most or all of their songs will often describe women (and black women in particular) in degrading and insulting ways.

It would seem that even more young women who are not blessed with 'James Bond girl' looks are striving for ultimately, unrealistic expectations in the hope of possibly settling down with and marrying a high ranking professional, such as a doctor or lawyer. All the while this is happening, many, many young men, more than ever in western history, are struggling to even go on so much as a date with a young lady. A growing phenomenon since the 2010s is occurring, whereby countless young men right up to their forties, are living lives that are not much different from their teenage years: many still living at home, shut in their bedrooms for hours on end, eating junk food, playing computer games, being glued to their social media accounts, listening to music, watching films and often watching pornographic content, day in, day out, with very little or no social life and with very little to look forward to, most of the year round. Many such, young men will sadly succumb to alcohol and/or drug addiction. According to a leading, US health expert, Surgeon General, Vivek Murthy, loneliness is as harmful as smoking fifteen cigarettes a day, with nearly half of all Americans in the early 2020s, being affected.

Low levels of self-esteem and self-worth will inevitability give rise to worsening, physical and mental health problems. Obesity, diabetes, heart problems, anxiety, depression, self-harm and thoughts of suicide. A vast array of talent and potential, going to absolute waste. So many young men who could and should have been professionals, tradesmen, husbands, fathers and role models, before they reached their 32nd birthday - If only mainstream society (that continues to fail them) and a loving, young woman had possibly have given them the time of day, when they were in their late teens to mid-twenties, instead of such women, continually rejecting them and selfishly chasing a pipe dream. As already mentioned in the statistics, young women are also more prone to physical and mental health troubles in earlier life, while spiralling in ever increasing debts from ever more, rampant materialism and consumerism to try and substitute their crushing loneliness, which many will ultimately be in denial about. Very, very few, so-called 'strong, independent women' will go through their years, never having to worry about the rent/mortgage and be able to fully enjoy a satisfying career, where she never faces any issues, within that thirty to forty-year, period of time.

A single, career woman is more likely to rely on welfare in mid to later life than a married woman. And very few, childless, career women who eventually opt to marry after their own fertile years have come and gone, will enjoy happy marriages. Toxic feminists will convince such women, that it is actually men who are solely to blame for their shortcomings, rather than admit that many of their philosophies and their ideals are deeply entrenched in flaws, convincing them that they are not accountable for any of their own, terribly poor, lifestyle choices. Countless women and girls in the western world are also drip fed such toxic nonsense by mainstream society on a regular basis.

It is hardly surprising then, that with militant feminism and uber woke ideals, infiltrating our places of education, work, our institutions and in some cases, places of worship, that there is a fast, growing number of men, feeling let down by modern society, with so many lacking decent, role models and to then be turned down by young ladies, over and over again, with even dating websites being of no help to their romance prospects. Many men pay considerable amounts towards subscription fees, year after year, often with nothing to show for it.

With millions more women focusing on chasing a career and trying to find a man of more high and economic status, leaving many, regular men, continuously single and frustrated, many will no doubt begin to harbour nasty and very unpleasant views towards women. And a fraction of such young men, will end up going down the slippery slope and become involved in the incel movement, where bitter tirades against women, many using explicit language and often referring to such women as '304s' – A code term for a vulgar slur, becoming the norm. Some will use phrases such as wanting to 'do an ER': a reference towards the infamous killer, Elliott Rodger, to the Chad's and Stacy's, at their college or workplace. Some will talk about which female celebrities and prominent figures are most 'deserving' of gang rape, torture and death.

Many incels will also argue that young women have never had it so good at any other time in history, with the said young women, being able to enjoy opportunities that their own great grandmothers, could only have dreamed of. Western women now outnumber men in higher education and for the most part, they have greater opportunities to work and travel abroad, have greater career and promotion prospects and are able to enjoy more social and leisure activities than women in pre-1980s times. For the incel movement, this adds insult to injury, fervently believing that modern women are continually ungrateful and take what they have and enjoy for granted, with many such young women, they believe, having a strong sense of entitlement and forever wanting more and more to fill a void in their lives, that in the end, they will ultimately never fill.

What an absolute mess!

While rich, powerful and influential men, seem to be more spoiled for choice with women, far more than ever before, many more single, everyday men, are very sadly being left behind and not given the time of day by the so called, fairer sex, in their own communities. Loneliness plays a huge factor in the mental health struggles of millions of people, both men and women. This looks set to rise even more. It is hardly surprising then, that more western men than ever before are willing to travel overseas and join the fast-growing phenomenon of men of all ages, ethnicities and backgrounds, known as the 'Passport Bros' movement in order to find a potential bride in Thailand, The Philippines, South American and former Soviet Union nations, where marriage, family and faith are deeply entrenched into the DNA of their cultures and way of life. In the huge majority of such marriages, men feel their wives are more loving, devoted and more appreciative than western women, especially if such women born and raised overseas, endured grinding poverty and were from a culture, where attitudes towards women in general, are not so pleasant. Men who look overseas to find marriage are often the subject of ridicule but usually, only by western women. (Many of whom are consumed with envy when they see such couples, enjoying strong and loving marriages.)

In July 1987, the world's population reached five billion people. Fast forward to just over thirty-five years in November 2022 and the world's population reached up to eight billion people. Much of this can be attributed to the many, large families of couples with four or more children in Far East and in Muslim majority nations, Birth rates among white majority nations are much lower in comparison. It would be fair to say that for the most part, that hypergamy has been a force for good in human history. Striving for betterment and the desire for one's own children and future grandchildren to not have to endure the hardships that they themselves, will have faced, is completely understandable. Those young women in history who left their family, friends and everything behind to marry men, who they knew were soon to be heading to a new country to start afresh, are to be truly admired,

During my visit to New York City in 1999, my Dad and I, visited Ellis Island, which was used as a procession station for the many millions of European settlers who arrived to begin new lives in the United States between 1892 to 1954. There were many unique, heart-warming and inspiring stories of men and women, with many arriving with their young children, some from the poorest areas with little money and little grasp of the English language, whose sons would later go on to start businesses, that would employ over a hundred people. It is these kinds of people that went on to make America the world superpower we see today. (I could have stayed at the Ellis Island museum all day, that day. It was one of the highlights to my visits to the Big Apple.)

Hypergamy becomes a curse when so many women strive to win over and marry a man of great power, wealth and influence and where the odds of doing so, are very incredibly slim. In this case, trying to win over and marry a highly wealthy and influential man. Even the best of professionals themselves, will have realistic expectations and will know exactly where to draw the line in what they can go on to achieve. For example, a skilled, English soccer player, knows that it is better to play and be loved by fans of a typical 'run of the mill' club in the top two divisions of the Premier League and Championship, such as Leeds United, Sunderland or Crystal Palace, rather than sign for the absolute giants of Barcelona or Bayern Munich and possibly run the risk of becoming a mere footnote, due to the fact that he will have to learn a whole new language very quickly, readapt to a new culture and new style of gameplay. The first team squad will be among the very best in the business. The said, signed new player, may end up as a substitute for most games, thereby, hampering his international prospects. (A professional soccer player career, lasts around sixteen years on average, with just eight years on average, being at his peak best. Therefore, he knows that he has to make the best with the finite time, that he has.)

The Greek legend of Icarus is also a great story about the risks of aiming too high. Icarus flew in the sky on makeshift wings, which he attached to his arms to fly like a bird. However, he flew too high and too close to the Sun, despite the warnings he was given, thus causing the wax, holding the feathers on to his wings, to melt away. Once, more than half of the feathers came off, the young Icarus crashed into the sea and died. It is therefore safe to say that realistically aiming to achieve better, within your means is a good thing and is always to be encouraged. But, to set the bar way too ridiculously high is way too risky – And in doing so, it may cost you dearly.

Imagine this awful scenario....

As mentioned earlier in this book, hundreds of thousands of serving, World War Two soldiers, after victory was declared against Germany and Japan, returned home to their sweethearts or fell in love, shortly thereafter to then enjoy long and happy marriages, with many lasting fifty years or more. These men often gave back to their communities, helping good causes and who often helped other military men who served in other conflicts, such as Korea, the Falkland Islands, Northern Ireland and the Gulf wars. Their loving and loyal wives, stood by their men, through thick and thin, with many of them having very little to begin with after the war and with many of their husbands, struggling with post-traumatic stress disorder, (PTSD) with the sounds of fireworks and a backfiring car exhaust, being enough to reduce them to shaking and being in tears.

But, what happened if say, most of these men returned home from theatres of war in 1945 to then discover that most of these women were not interested in them? What if many women, set their sights only on high ranking military men and those men, whose financial interests were not too badly affected, during the war years? It would be fair to say that, without the love of a good woman, the horrors of war, would have probably have got the better of most of these men and no doubt, many of them would have took their own lives or drank themselves to death before 1963 arrived. All of this in turn would have gravely damaged Britain's, post war recovery and morale. It is due to such men and women, along with the overwhelming majority of their children and grandchildren since, that the United Kingdom is for the most part, still a great nation. We must strive to make sure, more than ever, to truly honour those who fought against tyranny in the world wars and other such conflicts, that the western world does not collapse because of the 'bad apples' from within, encouraging thoroughly selfish behaviour, encouraging women via tacky, feelgood slogans to pursue unrealistic dreams and spouting poisonous ideologies.

PART THREE

CAN WE EVER GO BACK TO THE WAY IT USED TO BE?

The answer to that question, in terms of western world marriage rates and strong family units, ever returning to pre-1960s levels: it is highly unlikely indeed. Millions of women have been told since the sexual revolution, that modern feminism is 'liberating' them from being railroaded into what will possibly be, abusive and unhappy marriages for many, often for the rest of their lives, because it what their families and society, expects from them. The first generation of women who bought into this notion would have understandably, been seduced by such rhetoric. Many such women will have seen their mothers being beaten by their fathers, during their childhood years, for reasons, such as his dinner not being on the table when he got home from work, during times when their fathers were drinking too much and during arguments when money was tight for the family. These women and their siblings may also have endured physical and possibly, sexual violence from their fathers too. Why then, run the risk of allowing history to possibly repeat itself? Feminists need to realise that such marriages were among a minority, though it must be said, such marriages were indeed, more common in pre-1970s times, when general attitudes among mainstream society were different in regards to domestic violence, when the cries of a beaten woman, heard by neighbours, was seen as being none of their business and just one of those kinds of unpleasant things that happened now and then, akin to being woken up because of cats wailing and fighting in the middle of the night.

(Thankfully, attitudes have improved dramatically over the ensuing decades in dealing with domestic violence and most neighbours are more reluctant to call the police if they hear a woman's cries.)

The idea of becoming a 'strong, independent woman' is seductive. However, for the huge majority, whether they admit it or not, the dream will eventually turn sour by the time they reach thirty-five to forty years of age. Many of whom will face a life of poor mental and physical health, debt and despair. While some of their friends may end up divorced, those friends who are still married, will ultimately be far more-happier in life, with their children, enriching their lives. It is due to these factors, that very sadly, we are likely to also see a rise in female suicides in the years to come. Can modern feminists well and truly look at all of these millions of damaged, often masculine looking, deeply unhappy women, whose once pretty features are now long gone – Can they really look at their fellow 'sisters' in the eye and tell them that their beliefs and ideals, ultimately enriched their lives and the world for the better? It would certainly not appear to be the case. The overwhelming evidence is there for everyone to see.

What, if anything, can be done in order to reverse this tide of absolute, human misery by even just a small degree? Please remember that I am not telling anyone, man or woman, as to what they absolutely should and should not do. That is for them to decide. I merely provide the facts and give the best possible advice possible from the bottom of my heart and from my Christian faith. We must all face the very cold and hard truth, which will be a bitter pill to swallow for some....And, that is the fact that much of the modern, second and third waves of feminism has indeed, (as so many manosphere bloggers have mentioned, time and time again) ultimately failed women and many societies as a whole. Much of our institutions have declined in their standards, bowing to the altar of feminist driven, diversity and politically correct doctrines, in many cases, with certain institutions being a shadow of what they used to be. Those who question such doctrines are often met with hostility, including by uber left, media outlets.

Along with more growing numbers of men and women being lonely, depressed and single than ever before, divorces continue to rise, with courts far more inclined to support women and deny or severely restrict, even some of the best of these fathers, access to their children.

Many of today's children and teenagers are far more troubled and unhappier than they were in previous generations. It has now got to the point, where even many traditional, left leaning people: the huge majority of whom are decent folk and those most well known in politics and culture, men and women, who have played a huge part in helping to improve the lives of ordinary, working class people to improve legislation to fight the scourge of poverty and discrimination, over the years, are fast becoming disillusioned with the absolute mess that they are beginning to see all around them. George Galloway and the former Labour, Member of Parliament and former head of the Commission for Racial Equality, (CRE) Sir Trevor Phillips, a black man, are two big examples. (Sir Trevor Phillips, even once presented a Channel 4 documentary in 2015, titled: 'Things We Won't Say About Race, Which Is True.') Cassie Jaye, the director of the truly thought provoking, 2016 documentary-film, 'The Red Pill', focused on the manosphere movement from a feminist perspective. Ms Jaye eventually reached a conclusion at the end that will surprise those who watch it. That of which, I will not spoil it for you.

The ideals of modern feminism were created with obvious, good intentions. Those who fought vigorously for the rights to vote, to be given better access to education and opportunities, while helping to implement stronger legislation to further punish those who perpetrate, physical and sexual violence and abuse towards women and children, are to be fully recognised in the history books and applauded for their deeds. (Women from Emmeline Pankhurst to Rosa Parks to the 2014 Nobel Peace Prize winning, Malala Yousafzai: who, as a young girl, was shot and nearly killed by a Taliban gun man in Afghanistan for diligently campaigning for Afghan girls to be able to attend school.)

However, the downside from all of this has shown that the cure has now since, become even worse than the disease. A great deal of their feminist beliefs has in fact, caused a huge amount of damage to women, as well as men, in which any fourth, fifth or sixth wave of feminism, is certainly not going to resolve. Countless women have been falsely told over the decades, that marriage is 'only a piece of paper' and that the concept of marriage was 'invented' by 'religious zealots', going back, several thousand years ago to the desert tribes in the early times of the Old Testament, in order to hold women down to become slave like, baby machines. To cook, clean and obey their 'superior' husbands who owned them in the same way that they owned property, land and livestock. Women have also regularly been told the huge lie that abortion is 'essential healthcare' and merely a 'minor procedure', but which has of course, left a trail of psychologically damaged women in the process. Their mantra is to 'rise up' and be free, strong and independent from the 'toxic patriarchy' that has forever held women back since the dawn of time.

Sisters are doin' it for themselves – As the band, The Eurythmics, sang back in the 1980s. (A great and catchy tune, it has to be said.) As modern feminism began to take a stronger hold on everyday society, it must have been exciting for many women at the time, with a 'golden era' that was supposedly, looming on the horizon. In these current 2020s, it is crystal clear that no golden era has taken place for the so-called, strong, independent women. Nor will there ever be one. It is only by finally coming out of the state of denial and admitting the failings brought on by much of modern feminism, that we can then begin to implement any form of change. (In my 'Hidden Disabilities' book, I wrote a subchapter called 'The Culture of Denial', due to the fact many of those who have wronged, autistic and vulnerable people, cannot and will not, admit what they said and done, was wrong.) As we shall see from the following examples in history, that by admitting mistakes and acknowledging that certain ideals do not work, can we then begin to make any changes for the better.

The very basic ideals of communism were discussed by Greek philosophers, such as Seneca, back in the 4th century BC, but which were discussed in far greater detail by Karl Marx, in his book, Das Kapital – And his ideals and beliefs were of course, written with the very best of intentions to try and improve the lives of the downtrodden and hard up masses within society. While such ideals look good on paper and are effective to a very small degree, (eg: villagers, helping one another to get by) communism and its similar variants, certainly do not work in practice, when trying to run entire nations: the evidence of which is clear to see in various parts of the world, most notably, in the former, Soviet Union nations, which seen economic collapse, wars of all kinds, break out and the deaths of over one hundred million people, since the early twentieth century. The Soviet Union, eventually broke up, the 'Iron Curtain' fell in Eastern Europe, West and East Germany were reunified and the Berlin Wall was taken down. (Communist Yugoslavia also broke up shortly after, but which sadly led to bitter conflict, throughout much of the 1990s.) All credit must go to those leaders and politicians at the time, who faced up to the facts that communism, clearly was not working and who helped to bring in change to implement democracy within their nations. During my 2002 soccer trip, visit to Moscow, despite the fact it was a fascinating experience and that the Soviet Union had collapsed just over ten years before, the levels of poverty and hardship I witnessed there, were truly shocking. The living conditions in most of the city was not pleasant to say the least. Most of the cars on the road were dinky and many would not have been deemed, legally road worthy by British standards as they were literally falling apart. This from a nation which managed to put the first man into space and with a truly fearsome, defence and nuclear arsenal to hand.

The Volstead Act was another huge example in history, which ushered in the era of prohibition of alcohol, throughout the United States, after long, mounting campaigns from various, Christian organisations, which stretched back to the mid-19th century. Alcohol was seen as being among much of the main causes of much of early America's, social problems, leading to grinding poverty and violence in the home. This scourge, being typical among settlers from Ireland, Germany and Eastern Europe, including Russia. The Women's, Christian Temperance Union (WCTU) and the Anti-Saloon League (ASL) made great gains over the subsequent decades in swaying wider, public opinion and leading figures in politics. Prohibition, recognised as the 18th Amendment, eventually became law. It was firmly believed that the outlawing of alcohol, though it would be hard for some, would be an absolute blessing for all Americans in the long term and within a few years, would usher in huge, social changes for the better. But how very wrong these people were. The Prohibition era would in turn, give rise to large scale, organised crime, the likes of which had never been seen before in previous history, up until then, and much of which was spearheaded by the fearsome, Al Capone and other similar figures, either in or associated with, the Sicilian Mafia. Right from the very start, The Prohibition Act was literally impossible to fully enforce, with many hundreds of improvised and homemade, illicit breweries, throughout the country. From the inner cities to the remote countryside, there were countless, illegal drinking and gambling dens. Then there was the thousands of miles of border and coastline, with vast smuggling taking place, which regularly seen corrupt police and border officials being paid off by the mobsters. Vast quantities of beer were driven in from Canada, tequila driven in from Mexico, whiskey and stout shipped in from Ireland and rum shipped in from Cuba and the rest of the Caribbean.

After billions were spent on enforcing Prohibition, with little to show for it, the high levels of gangster violence, killings and injuries, and with no end to resolving the problems in sight, the American government eventually conceded defeat, finally coming to their senses and admitting that the Prohibition of alcohol, simply did not work. Alcohol was legalised once again, shortly after. It was also during the era of Prohibition, that hard drugs were also smuggled into America in large quantities for the first time, which in turn would herald the beginning of the international drugs trade, which in this current age, makes more money than both McDonald's and Microsoft, combined.

The other best-known example of an unworkable ideology: and one which was thankfully consigned to history by decent and sensible people, were the evil and racist, apartheid regime of South Africa and of course, America's own laws of segregation. In South Africa, many white people in the late 1940s were falsely led to believe, that the introduction of these restricting and segregating laws towards the majority black population were in the best interests of everyone, as living together or too close to each other was incompatible, especially as whites were apparently more 'civilised' and 'superior' than the blacks. Civil rights movements had achieved the abolition of segregation in America by the late 1960s. And with the growing, civil rights movements in South Africa, combined with growing support from white, Christian allies, famous people in music and entertainment and with the growing, international condemnation from across the world, with numerous nations, imposing sanctions on trade and commerce, even many of those in the then, all white, South African government, including those who had grown up knowing nothing else except Apartheid, knew deep down, that it was a system that was both wrong and unsustainable. It was for this reason, that Nelson Mandela and other, senior figures in the African National Congress, who for years, had been incarcerated at the brutal and harsh, Robben Island prison, were transferred to a specially, designated section of Pollsmoor prison in Cape Town, which had more comfortable facilities and conditions, to begin talks about dismantling Apartheid and ushering in a new, non-segregated democracy. As negotiations gathered momentum, Mandela was transferred to a prison which had a specially built house within its grounds to help him (and his comrades) to readapt to regular life, before he was eventually released in early 1990, with Apartheid ending, shortly after and with numerous changes taking place, including a change of the national flag. Nelson Mandela himself became the national president in 1994: something that would have been completely unimaginable, just twenty years earlier.

Could you imagine how utterly devastating it would have been, had the Prohibition Act, communist era, Soviet Union and Apartheid/US segregation, all lasted for another ten years? To be honest, it does not really bear thinking about. Only by fully admitting that certain ideologies and methods, clearly do not work in the long run, whether implied with good intentions for all of the populous or not, and with all the evidence available to back the case, can we then begin to implement, much needed, changes and reforms.

> "You can fool all people, some of the time and some people, all the time. But you can never fool all the people, all the time." – Abraham Lincoln.

Along with the overwhelmingly, large majority of men in Britain and beyond, I have no issues with women seeking careers and wishing to better their life's chances. And I truly wish them the very best of luck. However, though this may be an unpopular opinion in today's materialistic and secular age, women and girls should always be strongly encouraged to marry and have children, above all else. Encouraged by mothers, fathers, brothers, sisters, and all female, friends and relatives. But is this just too 'old fashioned' a prospect, in this fast and ever-changing world, to encourage as many young women, mainly within the twenty-one to twenty-six years age range as possible, to marry and settle down, from now on? And is this, as so many feminists will be eager to tell you, that marriage is simply a construct to hold women down, simply for men to control them and to imply that men, in the eyes of God, are in fact superior to women and are therefore justified in their view in how they control their wives and daughters in some cultures?

The following, brilliant video transcript was made by Brett Kunkle of California USA in February 2016, and is featured on the 'Stand to Reason', Christian organisation website, when he was challenged by someone who felt the Bible had quoted that men are indeed, superior to women. He then gave this fantastic response:

This week's challenge: The Bible says that men are superior to women.

A little controversial in this day and age. What does the Bible say about men and women and husbands and wives and their value and their roles? This challenge sites Corinthians as an example of a passage where you have men superior to women. I want to say a couple of things.

Number one: The key passage in Scripture on the value of human beings in Genesis 1: 26-27. That's where we derive human value, not on gender, not on ethnicity, but on the fact that every human being is made in the image of God. It says, "Male and female, he created them." (NASB1995) So, men and women are made in the image of God. In the Christian worldview, this is where we derive the value of human beings. Therefore, human value is intrinsic, and it's inherent to being human. If you're a human being, you are valuable. That's where we get our value, and so that's the foundation of biblical texts.

Now we come to the New Testament. We do see a distinction made between men and women. There's a passage that talks about men—husbands—being the head of their wives, and so a lot of people today look at that and go, "What does that mean? Doesn't that mean that men are superior to women?" Well, no, it doesn't. It's just referring to different roles that we have. There's a difference between having a role and having higher or lower value. They're not the same thing.

In fact, God models this for us. Look at the Trinitarian view of God. Father, Son, and Holy Spirit are all equally God. None is inferior to the other. Amongst the Trinity—Father, Son, Holy Spirit—there are different roles they play. So, it wasn't the Father who died on the cross; it was the Son who died on the cross for the sins of humanity. It's the son who says that he willingly submits his will to the will of the Father. Does that mean that the Son is somehow inferior to the Father? No, of course not. It's just a difference in role. The Son willingly submits himself to the Father, and that is key for our view of husbands and wives.

In fact, I want to take you to a different passage, Ephesians 5. Chapter five is a key passage. It will help us understand a little bit more about this headship, about the relationship between husband and wife. If you look in Ephesians 5 starting in verse 21, it says, "And be subject to one another in the fear of Christ," or to "submit to one another in the fear of Christ." (NASB1995)

First off, there is mutual submission that should happen in a relationship between husband and wife. The next verse, 22: "Wives, be subject to your own husbands as to the Lord, (23) for the husband is the head of the wife as Christ also is the head of the Church." (NASB1995) There is this idea of headship, or leadership, that a man has in a marriage relationship with a wife, but what does that look like? When we think headship, we think leadership, we think worldly view, right? "Well, I have authority over you. I tell you what to do. You listen to me. I give you orders." That's not the biblical view. That's not the model of Christ.

In Ephesians 5:25, we see this command to husbands: "Husbands love your wives." How? "Just also as Christ loved the church and gave himself up for her." (NASB1995) That's a tall order for husbands, right? Husbands are to love their wives, lead their wives, in the same way Christ loved the church. How did Christ love the church? He sacrificially lived his life and gave his life up for the church.

That's the role of the husband. That is a huge tall order. So, there's nothing in Scripture about men being superior to women. There's equal value with men and women. There are just simply different roles that men and women have in a marriage relationship. Different roles do not equal different value. Men and women are equally valued.

In fact, if you look at the origins of Christianity in the society that Christianity springs up within, you know that women are second-class citizens, third-class citizens. But Christianity dignifies women all throughout Scripture and gives them a whole different status. It's actually Christianity that brings the value of women to the forefront. So, does the Bible teach that men are superior to women? Absolutely not.

Hoping that this will clear things up, in regards to how God Almighty created men and women, in that we are equal but have various, different roles to play in life. There needs to be a global, 'better off this way' campaign by all denominations to strongly, encourage marriage, which will be very unpopular in some quarters, but the next generation, including children, need to be made fully aware that all other alternatives, as has been proven for some considerable time, will eventually lead to unhappiness and failure. There are countless 'memes' online, with tasteless cartoons, displaying images of 'mad, cat ladies', who spend their typical days with their hair unbrushed, curled up on the sofa, drunk from boxed wine, in their dressing gowns, thinking of how life could have been, being in a loving marriage to someone. However, this really is no laughing matter. These are our sisters and daughters, who for too long, have long been deceived by the 'career first, have fun, marry the handsome gentleman, more later on' Disney, fairy tale. I would truly hate the thought of any possible, future granddaughter of mine, ending up this way.

Truly loving, Christ centred marriages and having families by the age of twenty-six, for men and women, are by far, the best way forward – And the overwhelming evidence is truly clear to see among the many millions of such couples from across the world: from Malmo to Montevideo, Atlanta to Auckland, Belfast to Brisbane. If there were a sharp rise in Christian marriages, it would almost certainly, encourage many more such couples to turn to God, marry and settle down. The happier and content people are, the greater likelihood that they will be healthier and more productive members of society. It is a win-win for men, women, their children, church and community. This is what the Lord ultimately wishes for everyone. It is hardly surprising then, that marriage is mentioned so very frequently, throughout the Bible, in both the Old and New Testament.

> And the Lord God said, It is not good that the man should be alone; I will make him an help meet for him. (Genesis 2:18 KJV.)

WHAT WOULD JESUS MAKE OF ALL THIS?

> Nevertheless, to avoid fornication, let every man have his own wife, and let every woman have her own husband. (1 Corinthians 7:2 KJV.)

I think that, before we can begin to ask that question, we really need to ask as to why the manosphere movement even exists at all? Why was there no manosphere in 1900? Or 1950? Or even in 1976, when I was born? As already mentioned, the world has come a very long way in many regards, since the end of World War Two. However, since those dark days, it seems that both millions of men and women are becoming less satisfied in life and are unhappier than ever before, despite many people being more privileged, taller, fitter and healthier, than most of their forefathers ever were. Vast swathes of men are struggling to forge relationships and many of those who are in relationships, including marriages, feel deeply insecure and that things could come to an end at any moment, no matter how much they live by the rules, no matter how devoted and hard-working, that they may be. For far too long, women have been led to believe that there is always 'someone better' out there, if they are willing to look hard enough. For every woman who finds a man who is wealthier, kinder and better looking than the otherwise decent and respectable man she left him for, there are hundreds, possibly thousands more, who will go through the rest of their lives, never ever finding a better man. The good man she dumped, she could have spent many happy years with. Their great grandmothers, usually had far less, yet learned to be content with their lot in life. Their lives and those before them, were devoted to their husbands and children. And such men devoted their lives to their wives and children in equal measure. The lives of many such people were also devoted to their faith, church and community. Had it not have been for such amazing women, during both the world wars, so many surviving young men would not have got through the rest of their lives in the way that they did. Indeed, the same could be said of all wives, throughout the course of history, who stood by their men through thick and thin, in all wars, natural disasters, economic uncertainty, grave illnesses like cancers and many other, huge challenges and setbacks.

Many such couples may end up losing everything, including their children, during the most horrendous of times, but they stick together and soldier on throughout. It is a real triumph of the human spirit.

By diligently, promoting and encouraging, Christ centred marriages, more than ever before and giving such newlyweds the best possible help, support and advice to kick-start their new lives together, we not only honour God, we honour all of those who were less fortunate than us, who have since, come and gone, before us, such as our forefathers: many of whom endured grinding poverty that many of us cannot possibly imagine. Those, who endured disease and famine, the men who left loved ones to go to war, many miles away, but who never returned home, and the many millions of young women who were made widows because of tyrants, such as Napoleon and Hitler.

I truly believe that human beings of all backgrounds, colours and creeds, are hardwired by God for marriage. (One huge difference as to why we are wired so very differently from the apes, that human beings, certainly did not evolve from.) When British and European voyagers, ventured across the world and to some of the remotest, inhabited islands on the face of the planet, there were Kings and Queens, husbands and wives, among just about everyone, aged twenty-one and over. Some Kings, elders and tribal men of importance, had numerous wives. There is no culture, nation, county, island or principality anywhere on Earth, anywhere in history, where human beings can be found but where marriage does not exist. Even atheists and secular humanists get married. It is for this reason, that the act of celibacy among Catholic priests, monks and those who are indoctrinated to practice it, should be abolished, as it can cause grave, psychological damage, which can explain, though certainly not condone, some of the terribly high levels of child sexual abuse among a minority of priests, along with those placed in a position of trust, who commit such terrible acts, over the years. All churches must play their part in promoting and reviving marriage rates, and to also help them become more affordable, especially to financially struggling couples and women who are pregnant out of wedlock. Giving the best support possible, done with love and without judgement.

Jesus wants the very best, for both men and women.

No matter how much men have been repulsive towards women online and vice versa, no matter how unpleasant men have been towards women at work, in bars, clubs, in the street, and vice versa: Jesus is prepared to wipe the slate clean and forgive those willing to turn to him and repent of their sins.

Feminists.

Jesus fully understands the many grievances that women have and he knows that life is tough for hundreds of millions of women and girls, the entire world over. Unrepentant men (and women) who incite and commit physical and sexual violence towards anyone, will have to answer to God the creator, in the next life. Please be fully assured that God does not view any women any less, regardless of ethnicity of background, even though the culture and nation that they may come from, such as Iran or Afghanistan, may view women in a less than pleasant light. When it comes to the typical 'battle of the sexes' of regular, day to day life, Jesus does not take sides. There is never a case of Jesus demanding to women that they absolutely must marry before they reach twenty-five years of age, even if they do not want to or are not ready to do so. That they absolutely must have babies, look after them, cook, clean and give their husbands sex whenever they want. To never complain and always, always do as they are told by their husbands, as that is the 'natural order', the main purpose for their lives and what they are there for. Jesus never ever, says or implies this.

As pointed out by Brett Kunkle in his transcript: men are certainly not superior to women, though they have different roles to play and that men are the traditional head of the family, with Christ being the head of the Christian family. Any so–called 'holy man' or husband, who says that men are superior to women, truly dishonours the Lord. Men and women are certainly not the same but are valued by God in equal measure. Since the days of Adam and Eve, human beings have been given free will, which can be used for good and evil. While it is not a sin for a young woman to chase a career, first above all else, near the start of her adult life and to even renounce marriage, such a lifestyle will, in nearly all cases, see the said young lady, descend into a slippery slope, which will ultimately ensnare and enslave her, leading to sinful and destructive behaviour.

I strongly encourage any teenage girl or young woman to talk to any mature, Christian lady aged sixty or over, who was either brought up in a loving, Christian household or who has been a Christian for a considerable amount of years. These ladies will be able to strongly vouch, that to turn to Jesus, to stay at home with your parents, if it is possible, until your wedding day (as there is a far higher probability of descending into destructive lifestyles and behaviours when living alone) and to prioritise marriage over any career, is without a shadow of a doubt, the very best way forward. You will only need to look at many of these mature ladies to see that they look happier and healthier than most other, older people. They are far more likely to have happier and healthier husbands, children and grandchildren. Such ladies are not hard to find. There are probably a good few within a one-mile radius of where you live and who worship at the churches, closet to you.

> And ye shall know the truth, and the truth shall make you free. (John 8:32 KJV.)

These amazing ladies will be best placed to explain to young women and girls, as to why much of modern feminism has been an absolute disaster. Jesus himself, will say the exact same.

And to those most extreme and man hating of feminists who tell girls of school age in so-called 'debates' that they should become mothers, but that they 'do not need a man in their lives', who are very willingly, playing a part in trying to dismantle the traditional, family unit and in telling girls that all kinds of families, including single motherhood are equally as effective, and that there is nothing wrong with having an abortion: such false teachings, taught to impressionable young minds, will incur the wrath of God in the next life.

Incels. (Also including unpleasant elements among MGTOW, PUA and red pill communities.)

Jesus certainly does not approve of those who hold the deepest, hateful and misogynistic views on chat forums and of the online bile that is sent to women: be they girls at school/college, female colleagues at work, famous women in politics, entertainment, sports or anywhere else – Especially the extreme messages that involve threats of rape and murder. Jesus clearly understands that loneliness and continual rejection is both very unpleasant and bitterly frustrating, hence why marriage and starting a family among young adults, should be strongly encouraged, far more than ever before. Hate is never the answer and such prolonged bitterness can ultimately lead to violence, as has been seen in the case of Elliott Rodger, Alek Minassian and similar, incel killers.

In the film, 'American History X', after sustaining a terrible attack in prison, the lead character, Derek Vinyard (Edward Norton) is visited in the infirmary by his former school principal, Dr Bob Sweeney. (Avery Brooks) Derek became a neo Nazi skinhead, shortly after leaving school and had tattoos of swastikas and other far right imagery, adorned on his skin. Principal Sweeney is a black man in his mid–fifties. Most people in the position of Dr Sweeney would not have cared less for someone like Derek. However, he remembered how incredibly bright and talented his student was, during his school years, before his descent into extremism. After engaging in talk with Derek, (who was already starting to become disillusioned with his views, while serving his time and had even befriended a black man he had to work in the laundry room with) Dr Sweeney asks him a simple question, in regards to his extreme beliefs, during the conversation, which becomes a major game changer: "Has anything you've done, made your life better?" He had done numerous, terrible things, since leaving school, seen earlier in the film. It was at this very moment that Derek renounced his views and after his release, helped to encourage his younger brother Danny, (Edward Furlong) to renounce his own extreme views.

Derek, being helped and mentored by his former principal, does have very striking similarities to 'The parable of the prodigal son' told in the book of Luke 15: 11–32, and I have wondered if the writer and director of American History X, Tony Kaye, had the parable in mind when he wrote that particular scene? Likewise, Jesus would ask that very same question to members of the incel movement and other, extreme elements within the manosphere communities. He would also ask *"How would you feel if anyone wrote such terrible things about your mother, sisters and other female relatives, that are dearest to you and sent such messages to them on a regular basis?"* God will remember each and every, malicious act of trolling, each message on every forum and social media platform: each and every threat of rape and murder, even if done purely for the so-called 'lolz' – For cheap laughs and to gain attention. I cannot emphasise how incredibly serious, that this is. Only by repentance, turning to Christ and renouncing such abhorrent and sinful behaviour, can the slate be wiped fully clean.

In American History X, Dr Sweeney didn't see Derek as a Hitler worshipping thug, who was beyond redemption, like everyone else. This, despite Derek's crimes and the truly horrific way in which he killed one of the black men, trying to steal his truck, that was parked on the drive of the family home, which lead to his incarceration. Dr Sweeney, seen a bright boy who was led astray and who became embittered, after his father (a fireman, who harboured racist views) was killed by black thugs. Jesus too, remembers the bright boys that the overwhelming majority of those in the incel/extreme misogynist movement were – And still are, deep down. I hope and pray that as many as possible will renounce their ways. And those that do, will eventually, find a nice young lady to share their lives with. Those who do turn to Christ and who renounce their terrible views, would no doubt, make for good husbands and fathers, if they were given the chance. I hope and pray there will never be any repeat of any Elliott Rodger style attacks, in the future.

During an interview with Piers Morgan in September 2022, the world renowned, Canadian academic, Jordan B. Peterson, began to cry, after it was mentioned to him, that he was quoted by the film director, Olivia Wilde as being a 'hero' to the incel community for admitting to supporting, disaffected young men. (One of the main characters in her film, 'Don't Worry Darling' was loosely based on Peterson.) He replied:

"Sure, why not…It's very difficult to understand how demoralised people are, and certainly, many young men are in that category. You get these casual insults, these incels — what do they mean? These men, they don't know how to make themselves attractive to women who are very picky, and good for them. Women, like, be picky. That's your gift, man. Demand high standards from your men. Fair enough. But all these men who are alienated, it's like they're lonesome and they don't know what to do and everyone piles abuse on them."

Asked why he became so emotional at that moment, he then replied:

"It's really something to see – Constantly, how many people are dying, for a lack of an encouraging word – And how easy it is to provide that, if you're careful. You give credit where credit is due, and to say, you are a net force for good if you want to be." Such sentiments do ring very true. A simple chat to someone, being friendly and non-judgemental, can indeed, make a huge difference.

The mainstream, Manosphere movement.

Having spent many hours going 'down the rabbit hole' as it were, watching literally hundreds of online videos, including numerous documentaries, over the past two years at this time of writing, with many, very intense and emotional discussions, some often involving both men and women on the online platforms, covering a large array of topics on relationships, family, lifestyles, society, finances, health and fitness, among others, with opinions among both hosts and guests, often being controversial and uncomfortable – I would go as far as to say, that Jesus would certainly agree with the majority of what the most well-known, mainstream bloggers and influencers at this current time, have to say on their discussions and what they talk about, probably by around 75%–80% on average. Some, he will agree with, more than others.

The hundreds of online videos about getting your life and finances together, building strong families and communities, going to the gym, taking pride in your appearance, staying away from a life of crime, avoiding drugs, pornography, gambling, and excessive alcohol use, while staying away from a troublesome woman who will drain your time, energy, money and resources and finding a suitable partner in life who will be a positive force for good and who is far more likely to be loving, loyal and supportive throughout: I personally, cannot but help take my hat off to such people, regardless of how brash and aggressive that some of them may be at times, combined with their flamboyant swagger and with some regularly showing off their expensive homes, cars, watches, etc. Many such bloggers have received countless messages from viewers, mainly positive, with being told that they have changed their lives for the better. It is not surprising then, that figures, such as Andrew Tate, as controversial as some of his viewpoints most certainly are, have ultimately, struck a chord among so many millions of men and boys of all ages, from all walks of life in over a hundred countries across the globe.

If you were to take a Venn diagram to display Judeo-Christian values on one circle and the mainstream manosphere movement on the other, both circles would undoubtedly, overlap each other by a great deal. It is not that surprising then, that numerous, American pastors and people with very strong, Christian beliefs, have been involved with the movement and have been guests on platforms and speakers at events. (There are also some Muslim, manosphere bloggers, some of whom operate from studios based in Dubai.) A strong and happy marriage in particular, can have a very positive impact on so many others.

The Old Testament book of Proverbs talks extensively about evil women and bad wives who regularly make lives for their husbands and children, a total misery:

> A virtuous woman is a crown to her husband: but she that maketh ashamed is as rottenness in his bones. – (Proverbs 12:4 KJV.)

> Every wise woman buildeth her house: but the foolish plucketh it down with her hands. – (Proverbs 14:1 KJV.)

There are some 'grey areas' within the mainstream elements of the movement, in regards to avoid dating single mothers altogether, those who may have some unresolved 'Daddy issues' and other issues that they need to deal with. On some platforms, some of the hosts believe that it is not possible for any man to be merely friends with anyone of the opposite sex at all, with some proudly admitting that they have no female friends. Myself personally, I believe it all varies on the women themselves, the calibre of a young woman's, male friends (if there are too many, close male friends, it would be fair to say it is a red flag in that regard) and the kind of person that her own Father is. If the said friends, are all firm believers of the faith, then it should not be too much of an issue. Some argue, that women should not be allowed to enter the military and certain professions, as they are deemed to be far less reliable and who make life for their male colleagues, much more difficult. Yet another, bitterly divisive subject, with such sentiments made by male, professional colleagues who tell manosphere bloggers this, while remaining anonymous. Then there is the belief that many non-white women, often get hired by firms for certain jobs in more urban areas, simply for the said firm to tick the 'equality and diversity' box, rather than hire the usually better qualified, male applicant for the same position. There is also the theory that a small minority of women in the workforce also have a high tendency to make regular complaints and even take their employers to court. This, being a direct a result of toxic feminism.

At the worst end of the scale of the mainstream movement, the least unhealthy 10%, will be the expletive ridden rants about certain, famous and influential women who 'deserve' the online abuse they receive, who are sometimes referred to as pigs and dogs and who are portrayed as such in memes and cartoons, rants about 'post wall 304s', the 'horrible, Karen types' and the 'discussions' about the types of women who 'belong to the streets' via their own, terrible lifestyles. There are a hardcore of black manosphere bloggers who strongly urge all their followers, regardless of ethnicity or skin colour, to avoid relationships with black women altogether, due to the fact that black women are, in their view, 'typically difficult and troublesome' and who often, deliberately 'trap' young men into getting them pregnant. Hence, why they themselves, usually date only white, Latino and Asian women and encourage their black followers to do the same. There are countless millions of black girls and young Christian women, who will make for fantastic wives in the future. This strongly needs to be taken into consideration.

It is very understandable that emotions are often very high in many of the blogs and videos, regarding the state of modern, twenty-first century lives and relationships in western countries. Tensions are known to boil over on some platforms where men and women are present. A small minority of the expletive ridden rants could even possibly, reinforce the unpleasant views held by those in the incel community and those men who harbour negative views on women in general. Whatever the arguments and grievances that may be discussed and argued online, those who regularly contribute to the less savoury elements of the mainstream manosphere, seriously need to be more careful with some of their rhetoric at times. In an ideal world, there would be no manosphere or feminist movements.

Jesus said, I am THE WAY – Not, 'I am one of the ways.' By strongly encouraging faith, marriage and family, can we truly embrace going the best way, that there possibly is to go.

FIGHTING THE SCOURGE OF PREDATORS. (AND THOSE WHO ENABLE THEM.)

In Britain, some 1.2 million women and 700,000 men will experience domestic violence each year, according to the Office for National Statistics. Two women are killed on average by a current or former partner, every week. (Domestic violence rates increase sharply, during major, sporting events and fixtures.) In England and Wales alone, one in every four women will have been raped or sexually assaulted as an adult, one in six children have been sexually abused and one in every twenty men have been sexually assaulted as an adult. The emotional and psychological toll that this will take on survivors is enormous, with many succumbing to an array of mental health issues, addiction and with some descending into a life of crime in some instances. The costs to the taxpayer in terms of policing, hospitals, the judicial system, prisons and social care, goes up into the billions, every year. These statistics, as shocking as they are, will pale in comparison to dozens of other countries, across the world. These types of crimes are nothing new and very sadly, have been present in every nation and culture, throughout history. Although we cannot stop every single crime of this nature from taking place, we can certainly play our part in educating our young: not just on treating others better, regardless of our differences, but to also help them to spot the 'red flags' when there is a huge likelihood of the risk of potential danger. As well as the world's population rising sharply over the past half century at this time of writing, there is also a higher ratio of evil, sexual predators, with more now than in any other time in history.

Thankfully, in contrast to this, there is still an enormously high ratio of very loving and protective fathers and male relatives out there. Many of them are also very 'clued up' in regards to the fast changing, modern dangers of the current world. In the first instalment of the 'Taken' movie trilogy, Kim, the daughter of the main character, Bryan Mills (Liam Neeson) and her friend are both kidnapped by Albanian gang members, shortly after arriving in Paris. Mills, is a former CIA agent and he uses his 'unique set of skills' to try and rescue them. This scenario is every mother and fathers, worst nightmare. The first film was a total success, especially in how its gripped viewers in watching a loving father going above and beyond in order to try and save them. Prior to their Paris trip, the out of touch, ex-wife of Bryan Mills, married to a multimillionaire and living in grand luxury, continually moaned at her ex-husband, telling him that he was way too overprotective of Kim, regularly patronising him, that his former profession had made him paranoid. He was not made aware until after reluctantly signing the legal papers, allowing the then seventeen-year-old Kim, to be able to travel abroad, that Kim and her friend would also be travelling across western Europe to watch the U2 band on tour, which

Bryan's ex-wife did not disclose to him. Kim herself, was not made aware until reaching their destination in Paris, that the cousins of her friend, who were occupants of the apartment they were staying at, were away in Spain on holiday, leaving them totally vulnerable. The supposedly, friendly, young Frenchman, who shared a taxi with them from the airport into the city, was in fact, a scout for the gang members. Right from the very start, Bryan Mills could see numerous red flags, whereas his ex-wife, could not. Many millions of men are not given enough credit for the fact that they would be willing to sacrifice their own lives, in order to protect their wives and children. And they should indeed, be prepared to do just that, if such a situation were to arise.

The following is from Pastor Michael Foster of Ohio, who is a regular speaker at 21 Studios conventions:

"What is the reason 'women and children get off the sinking boat first? Is it that men are the disposable sex? No, it's because women and children are central to a man's (and his brothers) mission and legacy. Mission is indispensable. It's a spiritual and biological drive which burns in the heart of every healthy man. Therefore, men are willing to die for their legacy. This is the same reason a mother will throw herself in front of a bullet for her children. It's not that she is disposable. It's for the mission and the legacy. It's for the future. Both sexes want their 'fruit' to remain and mature. You can think of legacy as part of your mission that continues on into the future, through your progeny, through children and grandchildren

and great-grandchildren. So, legacy is the culmination of your mission. And therefore, if the house is on fire, you run in through the flames to get your kids. If the boat is sinking and there is only so much room, you give it to them. If there is an enemy at or in borders, you put your family somewhere safe, grab your weapons and lay down life if necessary. It's our legacy which is disposable. Just remember, you can't die for a legacy that you won't live for...get to it."

Coach Greg Adams regularly quotes that a good father will prevent his daughters from 'entertaining' people at sleazy clubs and prevent his sons from ever serving time behind bars. Indeed, such fathers will not stand by and watch them descend in to any form of ruin. As draconian as this may seem to some people, teenage girls and young women should be very strongly discouraged from going out at night, wearing very little and/or revealing clothing by fathers, families and peers alike. And, also to be strongly advised, that under no circumstances whatsoever, should they ever return to the home or hotel room of any man: even a man they happened to have known for a while, or a man, who is reassured by her friends that he is a 'nice guy' that can be fully trusted. (Or vice versa, invite the man to their home or hotel room.) Neither, under any circumstances, should they get themselves intoxicated to the point where they leave themselves vulnerable and at greater risk. All young ladies enjoying a night out, should agree to meet at a certain, less busy section of the club (usually the foyer) on the stroke of every hour/

half hour, should they lose each other in the crowds and have bad signals on their phones. If a woman is separated from her friends for more than half an hour then they are not exactly, decent and responsible friends to have. There is absolutely no excuse for this, whatsoever. Young ladies who are responsible, will all promise to enter and leave the club, together. The only other people they should agree to leave with, are other female friends that they meet there. There is greater safety in numbers. The huge majority of sex crimes, committed on weekend nights are actually preventable, with simple and sensible measures, put into place.

In December 2022, Channel 4 (UK) broadcast a hard-hitting documentary – Dispatches Undercover: Sexual harassment: The truth. In the programme, the presenter, Ellie Flynn, pretended to be drunk and 'separated from her friends' on separate evenings, in Liverpool and Central London. In both cities, within minutes of leaving her hotel, whilst sitting down nearby and minding her own business, she was approached, pestered and followed by men with less than pleasant intentions, despite the fact that she repeated in a slurry voice, that she wished to be left alone. One such man followed her all the way back to her hotel room but he quickly made his excuses and left, when she stated she was in fact, sober and questioned him as to why he entered her room without her consent, after her camera crew and security detail, who were very close by throughout, then turned up. Despite this, Ms Flynn was understandably, shaken by those experiences. Perhaps, one of Andrew Tate's most controversial sentiments, is that women should 'bear some responsibility' if they end up in such a terrible situation after a night out, whereby she drank too much, wore too little and in many instances, was unable to make clear decisions. If a man were to walk down a street in one of the most crime ridden areas of London or New York at night, with over a thousand dollars/pounds in his wallet and also wearing an expensive, Rolex watch, he would indeed, be deemed irresponsible for doing so and would be granted no sympathy for his foolishness, if were he to be badly beaten and robbed of them. This concept, however, is not seen as acceptable by many when it involves the subject of inebriated, scantily clad women who end up alone at night. More honest and frank discussions are badly needed by parents and peers alike, to warn girls of such dangers.

Going back to the 1950s, the huge majority of Britons were smokers. In this current age, smoking Britons, amount to just under 20% of the population. Children and teenagers are far more educated and aware of the health risks, associated with smoking than previous generations of pre-1960s times were, at their age. It is now far less, socially acceptable while, also, along with the rising costs of cigarettes, (including cigars and other forms of tobacco as a whole) combined with ghastly images adorned on cigarette packaging, of rotten teeth, of amputated legs – being reduced to stumps, and of blackened lungs, of various, different, heavy smokers, combined with messages in bold lettering, urging first timers not to take up the habit, children and teenagers are now far less likely to ever try them. These tactics, along with supermarkets and shops keeping cigarettes in cabinets, behind a shop worker at a till, which are now kept behind sliding shutters, have proved to have been very effective.

Just like the harder hitting, anti-smoking measures, that have now been put in place, in these current, times, there should also be hard hitting campaigns in newspapers, magazines, street billboards, bars and nightclubs to make promiscuous behaviour, which has literally been encouraged by certain, irresponsible downmarket newspapers and magazines, over the years, far less socially acceptable. And to warn teenage girls and young women of the possible consequences of rape and violence. (There were similar posters to warn American, military men of the so-called 'good time girls', going back in the 1950s, who may carry sexually transmitted infections. However, the posters I am suggesting, would warn women of the dangers of irresponsible behaviour, during weekend nights.)

Imagine for example, if there were equally, hard hitting images as there are adorned on cigarette packets, but in this case, of young women, curled up on their beds, sobbing or soaking wet in empty bathtubs, sitting with their knees up to their chest, their heads bowed and wet hair at all angles and with their limbs covered in bruises, adorned with the slogan: 'Just because he treated you like a Queen tonight, it does not mean he will keep treating you like one if you leave the club with him.' Some people will indeed, find such imagery upsetting and offensive, and it is true that the overwhelming majority of men who go out at weekend nights, would never dream of carrying out such terrible acts. However, if such campaigns can save many lives from being destroyed, then that can only be a good thing.

The worst 5-7% of town/city centre bars and nightclubs for track records of drink spiking, drugs and sexual offences, should face heavy fines and six-week closures per year. Any bar and club that are still in that 5-7% category the following year, should face heavier fines and a ten-week closure. Should any bar or club still reside in the worst category on the third year in a row, they should lose their licence altogether and face permanent closure. If restaurants, cafes and takeaway outlets can face swift and immediate closures for having very poor and unhygienic standards, which could lead to serious illnesses to customers and staff alike, then nightclubs, bars and even festivals, should face far more tougher measures, should they fail in their duty to protect those who enter their premises.

Monies that are raised from the fines would go towards counselling and support for survivors of sexual violence. Any man with a history of sexual offences, should be given lifetime bans from town and city centres on weekend nights, with prison sentences given to those who breach these conditions, without very good reason. Everything must be done to better protect people, going out at night, which also includes the LGBT community. All women should be granted free travel on all public transport, between 10pm to 6am on any day of the week. Their safety is of paramount importance. Back in 2012, a young lady was refused travel on a late-night bus in Nottingham to return home to Mansfield for being just twenty pence short of her bus fare. This, despite her pleas with the driver. This poor, young lady, was later dragged away and subjected to a sickening, sex attack, while she waited for her mother to come and pick her up. Just what on earth was this driver thinking? And why did none of the other passengers on board that bus, not rebuke the driver and pay that mere twenty pence for her? It is absolutely beyond me; just how unbelievably heartless these people were. This must never be allowed to happen, ever again. Taxi drivers and police officers, (male officers should be more strongly vetted) should offer women a lift home if they are stranded, especially if they are left in a potentially, dangerous situation.

In early 2023, the British news headlines were extensively covering the story of yet another, Metropolitan (London) Policeman, David Carrick, who has been revealed to have had a truly terrible history of callous and unrelenting abuse towards women, spanning twenty years. He has since been given, numerous, life sentences. There were numerous, missed opportunities to bring him to justice, earlier, as was also the case with Metropolitan Police Officer, Wayne Couzens, who often regularly displayed lewd and unpleasant behaviour, before he went on to kidnap and murder Sarah Everard in 2021, stopping and falsely arresting her, as she was walking home after visiting a friend. For a long time, the culture within many police forces, jobs and professions, including the fire service, have tended to 'look after their own' when complaints and concerns have been raised about certain individuals, within their ranks. Many reforms are urgently needed in all professions to weed out predators, racists and thugs.

First time offenders of domestic violence, should be enrolled in mandatory programmes in order to hopefully kerb such behaviour from happening again. Those who refuse to comply or repeat their crimes, should face heavy fines and prison sentences. Any man or woman who commits crimes of a sexual nature with camera footage to prove it: at nightclubs, on trains, buses or anywhere else, should also face serious consequences. As for those who commit the worst of crimes against women and children: If I had my way, here in Britain, I would have 'supermax' style prisons, built on small and uninhabited, Scottish Islands. I certainly would not have an issue with imposing the death penalty, in some cases. Inmates would spend 22-23 hours a day in solitary confinement in mere, box sized cells. They would be provided with either a Bible or Koran upon request, but with very little else. Visits would be restricted to only a few, each year. Some would see such measures as harsh. Indeed, they most certainly are. Imposing such measures would act as a very strong deterrent to anyone, ever thinking of committing such heinous crimes and acts.

> And whosoever shall offend one of these little ones that believe in me, it is better for him that a millstone were hanged about his neck, and he were cast into the sea. (Mark 9:42 KJV.)

Everything must be done to protect others from those with less than pleasant intentions and to strongly punish perpetrators. This also includes women who make false allegations of rape and assault towards men and who are themselves, violent towards adults and children. Those who enable such terrible acts, should also be held to account. While everyday life may not be as tough for women here as they are in certain nations with hard-line regimes, (some of the said nations, at one time, even allowed for young women to study and wear moderate, western clothing) the grievances of women in so-called 'civilised' nations, are indeed warranted in so many instances.

We must ensure that the concept of marriage, despite the challenges that it will ultimately bring through the years, will be far more encouraged and appealing to teenage girls and young women, to be seen as the right choice, regardless of what many feminists or others may say, rather than marriage being viewed as the lesser of the two evils, to the alternative of regular 'dating' and staying single for the majority of a lifetime. Domestic violence, while still a huge problem, is thankfully, talked about and tackled, far better than it used to be, with a whole array of helplines and organisations, available to give support and advice. While domestic and sexual violence will never be fully eradicated, it is strongly advisable for both young men and women to spend at least two years, really getting to properly know each other, before ever deciding to get married.

Likewise, it is also best to steer clear of someone, if there are too many red flags for comfort, such as the boyfriend or girlfriend having a short temper, dishing out regular, verbal abuse, bullying and controlling behaviour. We must make sure that we can make life fairer and more tolerable for women and girls, with stronger vetting procedures for those who work among the most vulnerable. To strongly rebuke and punish, brutal and abusive fathers, brothers, boyfriends and husbands, and to rebuke and punish those who abuse their positions, such as sex predator bosses, colleagues and clients/customers alike, to ensure that absolutely no one, nowhere, no matter how powerful and influential that they may be, cannot ever get away with so much as one tenth of the crimes committed by the likes of Jeffrey Epstein or Bill Cosby, ever again.

The ever increasing, sexualisation of girls, is one of grave concern. Numerous, famous and influential women in entertainment and music, are not particularly good role models, much of the time, with many often wearing very little on their music videos and on the stage at concerts, with sexually provocative dancing and lyrics, during their performances. Critics of such celebrities are often dismissed as being 'old fashioned' and 'prudish' by their adoring fans. Their heroines are 'empowering' to them and, in their seriously misled view, they are empowering to all women everywhere. Very sadly, the consistent and ever growing sexualisation of girls, is creating an enormous, mental health timebomb, with more girls feeling ever more insecure with their bodies and looks. The harrowing, British television drama 'I am Ruth', (2022) which starred the Titanic movie actress, Kate Winslet, who plays the long-suffering mother of an emotionally damaged, social media obsessed daughter, (who is played by Ms Winslet's actual daughter, Mia Threapleton) laid bare, the huge damage that social media and the constant pressure for girls to look their best, is having on them. There were scenes of intense, screaming arguments and of injuries caused by self-harm, during the play. It has been known for some considerable time, that excessive phone and internet use on computers and tablets, among children, is causing damage to young minds, whose brains are still developing. Both mother and daughter, received many messages from concerned parents, who have faced similar, challenging behaviour from their own daughters.

This may a not a popular opinion among many, but I strongly believe that all smartphones should be banned for all under sixteens, for the sake of their mental health and general wellbeing. Most children should only be allowed to have the most basic of phones that can provide just calls and text messages only. This in turn, would make lives easier for parents, guardians and teachers alike, all while keeping children safe from ever growing, peer pressures of modern life, safe from violent and pornographic images, which are often readily available, via a few phone swipes, which many will become desensitised to, (some of whom may act out some of the awful things they see) and safe from the scourge of paedophiles and less savoury people, some of whom, often pretend to be children who are looking for new friends in order to groom their unsuspecting victims to try and meet them, later on.

Since the turn of the twenty-first century, it has now got to the stage that sex crimes committed by children has rapidly increased, with smartphones playing a huge role in these growing statistics. As is also the case with violence and even murder, brought on by petty, online feuds and arguments. The mental health among vast swathes of early, twenty-first century born children is of extreme concern, which is made worse by much of the doom mongering and scaremongering, media coverage, regarding numerous subjects. The tide needs to be turned on this alarming mess. In the meantime, much more still needs to be done by social media and tech giants in regards in improving online safety for children. A plea, that has been made by millions of concerned parents, since the early 2000s. The safety of our young and vulnerable should always be a priority over profits. There needs to be an outright ban on schoolgirls wearing make-up and for them to be issued with longer skirts. Those girls who make their skirts shorter by tucking them into their waistlines, should be issued with on the spot fines. Everything, absolutely everything, must be done to stop the ever increasing, sexualisation of girls for their own protection.

In spite of the far stricter regimes and cultures, seen in China, neighbouring, Central Asian countries, Muslim and Hindu majority nations, the overwhelming majority of children in such countries, enjoy a childhood, free from sexual imagery and pressures that many western children and girls in particular, often have to face. Teenagers and young adults from such nations are far more likely to save themselves for their wedding day, as is custom. All this in turn, will make their marriage stronger. The huge majority of marriages lasting thirty-five years or more, around the world, are to be found in such cultures, where faith, chastity and love, helps to build a stronger foundation for the family unit.

All sex outside of marriage is sin. And crimes of a sexual nature, even more so. The TV critic, Mary Whitehouse, as mentioned earlier, despite being mocked on a regular basis, was so right with her concerns of many young women, often being reduced to little more than sexual objects in numerous programmes and shows at the time. The general culture of that era, merely normalised much of the lurid attitudes and behaviour. It was not until the Jimmy Savile revelations were uncovered, did we learn of the enormous fallout, from those times, with many more people coming forward about Savile, his enablers, associates and other, well known, famous individuals. Police hotlines were inundated with calls from countless survivors, to tell of the abuse they had received from supposedly, respectable individuals, such as doctors, lawyers, teachers and people of all professions.

We must never allow for whole generations to suffer in this way, ever again. Hence, why we should all collectively, take a stand against what is happening now in the 2020s. With less-stronger, family units and more unhappier relationships, giving rise to increasingly, sexualised cultures and thoroughly warped ideologies, will ultimately, become an absolute, recipe for disaster.

Virtually all adults, throughout history, have been guilty of sexual sin at one time or another. From Old Testament Kings to American Presidents, which in some cases, can lead to violence and murder. Even the humblest of people can be driven to terrible acts when exposed to sexualised imagery for the first time. The Himalayan kingdom of Bhutan was the last country on Earth to have television made available to the public until 1999. This deeply devout, Buddhist nation, having less than a million people, and where crime rates were generally very low, had very little contact with the outside world, with many Bhutanese citizens, living lives, not much different from their ancestors. Contractors, involving engineers and technicians were brought in from neighbouring India's, 'Bollywood' industry to build and set up, Bhutan's, first television studios. Television sales were a huge success with televised, religious services and European soccer, being among the main reasons as to why people bought them. (During the previous year, France '98, World Cup, soccer fixtures were shown on large screens in the Central area of Thimphu, the capital city, which drew in large crowds and thus, further prompted the desire for television to be made available to the Bhutanese public.)

Very sadly, crime rates skyrocketed for a short while, many of a sexual nature, by men who did not even know that bikinis, short skirts, stilettos and even glamorous, blonde-haired women, close to six-foot-tall, actually existed, until such they appeared on their screens. While none of the channels, then or now, shown any pornographic content, much of what they had seen had certainly affected the minds of those who were not used to seeing even the mildest of sexual imagery.

Many actors, singers and entertainers, men as well as women, have gone on to express much regret, in regards to how sexualised, some of their shows were and of the lifestyles that many of whom, once led, at the height of their fame. The longest serving Editor of the now defunct, 'Loaded' magazine, Martin Daubney, has since to his credit, expressed deep regret, that the once very popular magazine during the 1990s, which featured interviews with some of the best names in music, sports, showbiz and culture (and for a time, was the shirt sponsor of the north London, soccer club, Barnet FC) sadly, ended up becoming little more than a seedy, soft porn magazine, while in a desperate bid to keep sales up, as more rival 'lads mags' began to emerge, in the early to mid-2000s.

Mr Daubney made a documentary for Channel 4 (UK) in 2013 titled: 'Porn on the brain.' This programme shown just how truly devastating that the multi-billion, pornography industry can be to those who are addicted to viewing regular content, with brain scans of addicts, showing abnormal, activities and deficiencies in certain sections. Many addicts claim to be regularly depressed, anxious and withdrawn, with some often feeling suicidal. Indeed, even on a spiritual level, excessive viewing of pornography as with fornication, is incredibly damaging and can affect our relationship with our Heavenly Father as well as our loved ones.

¹⁸ Flee fornication. Every sin that a man doeth is without the body; but he that committeth fornication sinneth against his own body.

¹⁹ What? know ye not that your body is the temple of the Holy Ghost which is in you, which ye have of God, and ye are not your own?

²⁰ For ye are bought with a price: therefore glorify God in your body, and in your spirit, which are God's. (1 Corinthians 6: 18-20 KJV.)

Celebrities, such as the former NFL star and actor, Terry Crews and the singer, Billie Eilish, can vouch for how damaging, excessive viewing of porn can be. All seedy, so-called newspapers and magazines that promote and literally encourage premarital sex are poisonous, with their regular and over exaggerated 'sex surveys' and they are best avoided at all costs.

> "Pornography is not a thing to be argued about with one's intellect, but to be stamped on with one's heel." – GK Chesterton.

MAKE MARRIAGE GREAT AGAIN

There are indeed, a fair few things that we need to try and make 'great again' if we are to have any hope of reversing at least some of the colossal damage being done all around us, before our Lord Jesus Christ returns and thus, ensuring that many, current lost souls as possible, will eventually be saved. Encouraging, Christ centred marriages among our young, many of whom, are having their impressionable minds poisoned on a daily basis, and warning them about such warped ideologies and influences, must be of absolute, paramount importance.

It is very hard to suggest what exactly can be done to reverse just a fraction of the vast, rising tide of loneliness and of the many, many unhappy and unfulfilling relationships that are blighting countless lives. However, I strongly believe that the church can play an active role in helping to bring people together, more than ever before, by arranging fortnightly, monthly or bi-monthly, singles activities and events, that are in fairly relaxed settings, in a non-judgemental atmosphere, which even non-believers and single parents would be welcome to attend. These can involve cinema trips, picnics in parks, dinners at restaurants and days out to beaches, forests and lakes. Churches can ask for annual fees of ten pounds, Euros or dollars and to implement some basic rules in which smoking and alcohol will not be permitted and any forms of bullying, persistent, blasphemy and/or bad language and unpleasant behaviour will not be tolerated, which would lead to swift removal from any groups, without a refund of the annual, membership fee.

Some will argue that such ideas are totally absurd and that churches are not dating agencies. However, if such schemes can possibly bring couples together and lead to marriages in the tens of thousands, then setting them up would be completely worth it. Churches of all denominations can play an active part in bringing others together. Many will argue that thousands of couples meet and fall in love in church anyway, while attending Sunday services and weeknight meetings, but this is not possible for everyone to achieve for a variety of reasons, especially autistic, physically disabled and vulnerable folk, who may struggle to socialise in larger and busier, group settings. Some singles groups and activities may be a total and complete success, while others may not fare as well and this will vary from place to place. Everyone aged twenty-one and over, of all ethnicities and backgrounds would be welcome. Only in extreme circumstances, should anyone be denied membership from the very start.

Younger and youthful, Christian couples, aged under forty, could play a huge role in helping to set up church led, singles groups: talking to the more-younger members about their own marriage and providing valuable, help and advice from their own life experiences. Any young, married, Christian man from a more-worldly background, would be in a more ideal position to discuss anything in regards to the entire, manosphere movement. The Bible places very strong emphasis on marriage and all churches must therefore, play an active role in helping to bring people together, more than ever before. There are so many people, living very busy lives and there are countless men, who invest large amounts of time and money, using online dating websites and apps with most having very little success or no success at all. Many people have stories of meeting places being too noisy, and of their dates being rude and obnoxious, with their body language being negative and with their dates continually, staring into their phones, throughout. Some will have been stood up.

Those organising such activities, should ensure that they are as friendly and relaxing as possible, free of loud music and hordes of hyperactive children, running about. While there is no caste iron guarantee that everyone will find the right match, such schemes will hopefully forge many new friendships and bring many others to faith: which in turn, could widen their social circle and possibly help them to meet someone special, on another occasion. Churches could indeed, make a fair deal of money from annual, subscription fees, should an average of thirty to forty people attend such events over any particular year. Any couple that do marry, through such a church led scheme, should be offered generous discounts for their wedding day fees as an extra incentive, to further promote marriage. At this time of writing, I am forty-six years old and have still yet to marry. As a child, I firmly believed that I would be happily married with three children, living in a nice house and with a decent car, before my thirtieth birthday. Just work hard, stay out of trouble and live by the rules, that's it. Or so I thought. Sadly, this never happened. I still hope and pray that the prospect of marriage and home ownership is still within my reach before my time on Earth is over. Churches of all denominations will garner far more respect from the general population and people of all different faiths and cultures, across the world, by doing everything possible to encourage and promote chastity and marriage, far more than ever before. Promoting, Christ centred marriages at each and every turn, regardless of any backlash from certain elements of society and the mainstream media, should be at the forefront of just about all churches, everywhere.

Do chastity movements really work?

Since the 1990s, there have been numerous movements to promote abstinence from having sex before marriage in the United States. The two best known among them is 'True Love Waits' (TLW) which was created in April 1993 by the Southern Baptists and which has a sizeable following, across the world. The True Love Waits pledge states:

'Believing that true love waits, I make a commitment to God, myself, my family, my friends, my future mate and my future children to be sexually abstinent from this day until the day I enter a biblical marriage relationship.' (Wiki)

Abstinence, also extends to pornography and sexual thoughts. The organisation has held youth rallies and music events across America, over the years. Over 102,000 young people made the pledge within the first year and this figure rose to 2.5 million, young Americans making this pledge by 2004. The huge majority managed to maintain their pledge and have since, enjoyed very happy marriages.

The similar, 'Silver Ring Thing' movement was founded in 1995 but have since, changed their name to 'Unaltered.' The organisation was for a time, funded by the US federal government. Silver, purity rings are worn by their adherents as a permanent reminder of their oath. Their theme verse is:

> "For this is the will of God, even your sanctification, that ye should abstain from fornication. That everyone of you should know how to possess his vessel in sanctification and honour."
> (1 Thessalonians 4: 3-4 KJV.)

These movements have been widely praised by leading religious and political figures but have come under strong criticism from much of the mainstream media and secular/atheist organisations, alike. Despite much of the success stories, abstinence movements struggled to make much impact in Britain and Europe, often becoming the subject of ridicule and seen as an

'Americanised' gimmick. Many teenagers on this side of the Atlantic, mostly girls who had already lost their virginity, had scoffed at the concept – That is until you asked them if they wished for their future daughters to do the same as they had done, when they grow up to become teenagers themselves. Girls in this regard, are far more likely to feel a sense of deep shame, than boys are.

> But the fruit of the Spirit is love, joy, peace, longsuffering, gentleness, goodness, faith, Meekness, temperance: against such there is no law. – (Galatians 5: 22-23 KJV.)

CONCLUSION

"This is a man's world. But it would be nothing, without a woman or a girl." – James Brown.

There is no denying that the manosphere movement has had an impact on tens, if not, hundreds of millions of men and boys across the world, especially since the mid–2010s. Many men have felt attacked by modern feminism and badly let down, not just by mainstream society, but also, in many instances, churches of many denominations. The very best aspects of the manosphere movement are virtually Christ like: a just and noble cause, by encouraging happier and healthier lifestyles. To stop having excuses for whatever is holding them back and urging men and boys to become the greatest man that they can possibly be, to be the best in their bloodline, to be 'based' - meaning to be confident in oneself and not care what negative people think. To break, continuous, generational curses, such as poverty and addiction, with the movement actually saving the lives of possibly thousands of men and boys along the way, who were apparently at their wits end and who were on the verge of giving up, because of the often harsh and brutal, stresses and strains of everyday life - And to also be decent role models to others by helping one another and giving back to their communities.

The very worst aspects of the movement and the incel subculture in particular, can be compared to a truly horrible creature, that has the jaws of a great white shark, the crushing abilities of a boa constrictor and the deadly venom of a western taipan snake. While Andrew Tate and the fifty or so, other most well-known figures within the movement have most certainly made a huge impact, leading to mixed reactions and discussions on the subculture, in school classrooms, offices, pubs and clubs alike – not to mention, even in the highest levels of academia on both sides of the Atlantic, it is fair to say that Andrew Tate is a hero to some and a villain to others. Whatever your opinion of him, there is no denying that he has most certainly sealed his place in the history books and becoming a cult like figure, similar to other notable individuals who continue to divide opinion: from Jesse James and 'The Wolf of Wall Street', Jordan Belfort. Both of whom stole huge amounts of money. The former stole using guns, the latter, while wearing a suit and tie. And from the fearsome Kray twins, (including one of their most well-known friends, Roy 'Pretty Boy' Shaw, who lived in my hometown for a while as a WW2 evacuee and who I just so happened to have seen, near the ringside, at a boxing event in East London, back in 2000) all the way up to the infamous, Colombian drug baron, Pablo Escobar. Thousands of people have made the pilgrimage to the resting place of Mr Escobar, over the years since, with many even snorting cocaine from his tombstone, as well as laying flowers and tributes.

Some of the views and opinions of Andrew Tate and the bigger names within the movement, will have undoubtedly, caused shock and offence to many. I do not agree with absolutely everything they say, though personally, cannot help but agree with the huge majority of their views.

Whether or not, Andrew Tate, his brother Tristan and/or any of his henchmen, will ever serve time behind bars, for having been found guilty of any trafficking and/or sexual offences, with overwhelming evidence available to prove that such acts were committed, (or that the Tate brothers were in fact, victims of a malicious, 'matrix' backed, smear campaign all along, in order to bring them down, silence them and to tarnish their reputations) still remains to be seen at this current time. Andrew Tate's viewpoints however, do seem to pale in comparison to the lyrics and views of certain musicians and entertainers, who have made a fortune from shocking and offending others, and who have been famous for much longer.

Over the years, there have been numerous figures in entertainment and music, most notably, rap artists, that have made a sizable fortune from belting out songs that often contain violent, misogynistic and deeply offensive lyrics. Many such songs have been around before the launch of the internet and when Andrew Tate himself, was a small child. Some of these rap artists, have not only have a large, female fanbase, some of them have also have also acquired the immense wealth of long-established musicians, whose fame began in the 1960s. (Rihanna, whose songs and lyrics are often sexually provocative, has become only the second, black female in history after Oprah Winfrey, to become a self-made billionaire.) And long before Andrew Tate and the main 'big guns' in the current manosphere were even born, there were a whole array of famous names that proudly boasted of their numerous 'conquests' with women: from Gene Simmons from the rock band, Kiss, to Mick Jagger and Keith Richards from the Rolling Stones. The long serving President of Cuba, Fidel Castro, has even made the bizarre claim of having bedded up to thirty-five thousand women!

Men of my father's generation would regularly hear of stories, throughout the Sixties and Seventies, about the excesses of rock stars and of their wild and fast living lives, the parties with 'groupies' and of 'rituals' that involved the trashing of hotel rooms and of television sets being thrown out of the windows. Those who lived to tell the tales of their most wildest days, who lived and enjoyed experiences that 99.99% of the world could not even begin to imagine, travelling to dozens of the greatest cities on Earth, (several times over in many cases) and performing to sell-out crowds in packed out venues: They too will admit that the happiest memories in their lives, were not of those wild times, but of those with their families and watching their children grow up, through the years. It is hardly surprising then, that the Rolling Stones wrote and sang: '(I can't get no) Satisfaction' – One of the bands most iconic tunes and one of the most iconic rock songs, of all time. King Solomon, who had great wealth, seven-hundred wives and three hundred concubines, wrote a similar and more detailed account, three thousand years earlier, about vanity and dissatisfaction:

> "Remember now thy Creator in the days of thy youth, while the evil days come not, nor the years draw nigh, when thou shalt say, I have no pleasure in them." (Ecclesiastes: 12:1 KJV.)

Much has changed in the course of my lifetime, especially UK society as a whole. Though there has been stages of progress in some ways, there have been more setbacks in others. As a child of the 1980s, growing up in southern England, racist and sexist attitudes were still very rife. Race riots and soccer hooliganism were a common feature on our television screens. A 'macho' and competitive culture was very evident in all aspects of everyday life. Snooker and darts tournaments, often drew in over seven million viewers, each time, with most players, regularly drinking and smoking, during games. Rugby matches were much more, bruising and blood splattered encounters, with deformed, 'cauliflower ears' being more common among players, back then. As well as sports, which included British wrestling on our screens, (none of our wrestlers were on a par with the likes of Hulk Hogan and Dwayne 'The Rock' Johnson, but watching them in action was good fun, nevertheless) and despite having just four terrestrial, television channels, during much of that particular era, our 'boxes' regularly featured programmes and films with 'manly' figures, such as John Wayne, Sean Connery, Burt Reynolds, Chuck Norris, Clint Eastwood, Oliver Reed and Richard Harris. The children of my generation also enjoyed American, action programmes, such as The A-Team and Knight Rider and we looked up to muscular figures, such as Sylvester Stallone and Arnold Schwarzenegger. Many of the comedies that featured on our screens, would not be acceptable by 2020s standards, because of the regular, outdated attitudes within them. The comedy character, Alf Garnett, (Warren Mitchell) the lead character of 'Till death do us part' and its later series, 'In sickness and in health' – About the life of an embittered, racist and sexist, East London pensioner, is another well-known example.

Discussions, in regards to wellbeing and mental health, were virtually non-existent, in those days. 'Real men and boys don't cry!' was a common mantra. And it is highly likely, that for this very same reason, not one person suspected that I could possibly be autistic. I 'looked normal' and was therefore, merely viewed as a naughty boy who just needed to be 'straightened out' from my regular and sometimes bizarre, traits and habits. Though the 1980s were far from perfect and despite the unpleasant revelations of some famous individuals of that era, that have since been brought to light, I cannot help but feel that, overall, there were far better role models within our communities and upon most of our television screens, for children and teenagers to look up to, than there are today. The boxer, Frank Bruno, Superman actor, Christopher Reeve and of course, 'Mr T': the actor of the A-Team and Rocky III fame, (real name, Laurence Tureaud) who is an ardent Christian, were fantastic, role models for children of my generation. Even cartoon characters, such as Optimus Prime from the Transformers and He-Man from the Masters of The Universe, as strong and mighty as they were, they were also very gentlemanly and chivalrous, throughout. (At the end of each, Masters of the Universe episode, He-Man and/or one of his friends would give a short talk, recapping certain scenes in that particular episode and emphasizing the need to be just, noble and kind towards others, whatever we may face in life….. Even when others are not so pleasant towards us.)

As the 1980s came to an end and the 1990s began, a growing army of feminists and 'do-gooders' started to complain at just about everything, which also included regular programmes, that children were watching on television, at the time. Wrestling and action-adventure programmes were apparently making boys 'more aggressive' in the playgrounds and while playing in the streets. This, was complete and utter nonsense of course, but much of the content was gradually being removed from our screens. Even stories and characters for more younger children were coming under fire. Thomas the Tank Engine was viewed as being 'bullying' towards his female carriages, Annie and Clarabel. Around this same time, the narrator of the show, (between 1984-1986) was the iconic, Beatles drummer, Ringo Starr. He himself, had never once complained about anything like this. The Beano comic was deemed sexist, as the mother of the front-page character, Dennis the Menace, would regularly prepare and cook homemade pies, while his father read the paper and smoked his pipe in the lounge. (Even though he was in a suit and had worked all day at the office.) Dennis himself, was deemed a 'homophobe' for sometimes picking on the genteel and effeminate Walter, who lived nearby.

The Punch and Judy, puppet show: a long-standing British tradition, spanning back over three hundred years, was not even spared, thus being deemed chauvinist, violent and misogynist, despite entertaining many generations of men, women and children, without anyone making complaints. Modern feminists and do-gooders, with too much spare time on their hands and with nothing better to do, would also regularly complain that there is not enough female, black, gay, lesbian etc, representation on television, which still continues to this day. Just about everything in life gets inspected under their social microscopes. The BBC, Britain's Channel 4 and numerous organisations of all kinds, seem to have a growing army of box ticking, 'diversity' jobsworths, who are usually paid, ridiculously high salaries. A televised, historical drama about Anne Boleyn, the second of King Henry VIII's wives, had Jodie Turner-Smith, a black woman, playing the lead role. (All the 'luvvies' who praised it and who dismissed any negative feedback, were then asked if they would be fine if a white actor such as Tom Hardy, were to play the role of Martin Luther King Junior? Alas, the response was met with silence.) It is because of politically correct driven zealots, that so many British and American television commercials, often consist of clumsy, white hipsters with flawless and goddess like, black or mixed-race spouses. The man is an overgrown child, who struggles with simple tasks, while she is a strong, empowering woman, who can do absolutely no wrong, whatsoever. There is a regular tendency via modern feminism, to continually make men look typically weak and lacking in confidence.

Modern feminism has not made western society any more-better, since the 1960s. Quite the very opposite in so many cases. The evidence is clearly there to see. There are now many examples of schools giving awards to children, merely for 'participation' and of many boys being feminised, being denied the chance to play traditional, boys sports/activities and being held back during their vital, school years, through no fault of their own. Many of their fathers who they were close to, have been unfairly denied access to them, via the divorce courts. Millions of men, who were without a father and/or any decent role model in their earlier lives, are far more prone than women and girls, to be trapped in a cycle of addiction, violence, prison, homelessness, mental health struggles and are more prone to suicide. (Men aged forty to forty-eight in Britain, are most likely to take their own lives and with North East England, having the highest rates.) Society often vilify and wash their hands of such men. These are the very men who are the backbone of the nation. They fight in wars, protect the public, work in tough, demanding and unpleasant jobs in mines, farms and factories, and build roads, homes, office blocks, and skyscrapers in all weathers. Many such men in tough, working cultures, are often far less reluctant to open up about any mental health struggles, that they may be facing.

> "Only women, children and dogs are loved unconditionally. A man is only loved under the condition that he provides something." – Chris Rock.

If millions more such men are also destined to go through the majority of their adult lives being lonely in the years to come, then the consequences will be nothing short of catastrophic. Many of the countless millions of surviving soldiers and civilians of the world wars in Europe and beyond: men and women, would not and could not, have got through the horrors of those awful times and rebuilt their lives in the way they did, without their faith in God and the love and support of their husbands and wives. The same applies to survivors of all wars and life changing events, throughout history. It is not surprising that so many marriages lasted forty years or more, with such couples raising great families and them giving so much back to their communities. Those couples who pull through in such times of adversity, have a very strong tendency to be more grateful for what they have and enjoy. In every nation, culture and religion, couples in long lasting marriages are generally held in higher regard for this, than for any titles or achievements to their name. The overwhelming majority of such couples in long lasting, strong marriages are often very respected and viewed as being more trustworthy and reliable. Those husbands and wives who destroy their marriages via cheating, (including even those who manage to save their marriages) are never held in the same regard, thereafter.

The Hollywood actor, Michael Douglas, after his role in playing a cheating husband in the 1980s movie thriller, 'Fatal Attraction', who then later, endures a terrifying, stalking campaign after ditching his impregnated lover, Alex Forrest, played by Glenn Close, was inundated with letters from married men, telling him that the film had in fact, saved them from having 'flings' with other ladies, such as their secretaries and the pretty, young barmaids they enjoyed flirting with, while out with their drinking buddies. It is fair to say that the film possibly saved hundreds of marriages from potential ruin. (The term, 'bunny boiler' was coined after a particularly, unpleasant scene in the film, which involved the killing and boiling of the family pet rabbit by the unhinged, spurned lover.) You never do find out at the end, whether the marriage of Michael Douglas's, Lawyer character, Dan Gallagher, ultimately survives or not.

The fallout from sexual sin leaves a devastating, ripple effect, often creating a chain reaction that can continue for months, and in some cases for years. Those couples that have had strong, Christ centred marriages, spanning decades, are truly among the most blessed of people and they are an inspiration to many. Those who lead so-called 'lifestyles' with continuous, drug and alcohol fuelled partying and casual sex, never fill the void that is consistent, throughout their lives. Some lives will be much shorter than others, through such excessive ways. Many British women, who believed they could work hard and play hard, just as much as men, and who embraced the hard drinking and partying 'ladette' and rave culture, week in, week out, during the 1980s, 1990s and 2000s, are now beginning to pay the price for their previous excesses.

It is for her strong faith, marriage and service to her people over the years, that Her Majesty, Queen

Elizabeth II, has rightfully earned her place in the history books as one of the most influential women of all time and hence, the overwhelming, outpouring of grief, of love and of the astronomical amounts of flowers and tributes, laid in nearby Green Park, after her passing, the likes of which I have never seen before and will never see again. Faith, marriage and the family are at the absolute bedrock of any, true, decent and functioning society, regardless of what anyone else may think. Many of us truly long for the good old-fashioned values, that were far more common in her earlier years, to be more common in this current era. What would have been seen as being completely abhorrent and totally unimaginable at the beginning of her glorious reign by everyone at the time, regardless of their views and political leanings, is now slowly becoming the norm in some quarters.

The most militant of feminists and woke zealots must therefore, never ever be allowed to win the ever bitter, culture wars. Many of their doctrines are harming so many of those that they purport to protect. They encourage boys to be more effeminate and for girls to be more masculine. Many are pushing the truly damaging agenda, that biologically born males can be women and are women. And vice versa. Some literally want for men and women to no longer be called, men and women and for both to be given different titles. Some modern, academic texts now even refer to women as 'birthing people' and 'menstruating people!' It really is verging on the ridiculous. This is something that is not to be disputed or questioned. How are biologically born females, supposed to compete against their trans rivals in sports, who are taller and stronger than they are? How can this fair and right? On a far more serious note, why should biological females be forced to endure the prospect of having trans individuals, share their restrooms and changing rooms, with them? Why should female prisoners, many of whom have been scarred from sexual violence in their childhood and/or adult years, with many having less than eighteen months to serve on their sentences, and who are strongly determined to make a fresh start upon their release, then be forced to share a cell with a trans inmate, thereby placing them at risk and possibly ruining their future hopes, while also undoing any progress they might have made? Those within the governments of uber liberal nations and US States, that will be or are strongly considering, pushing through any new legislation, to help further accommodate the 'needs' of the transgender community in these ways, without addressing the genuine concerns of biological females and their families, by merely dismissing them as 'transphobes' who need to be more tolerant in this current, modern age, will be enabling abuse towards the vulnerable. They truly will be on the wrong side of history.

Many teenagers and young adults have taken puberty blockers and similar, 'gender bending' chemicals, while also undergoing, grotesque surgeries, many of which are irreversible and can cause enormous, psychological damage to those who have undergone such procedures. According to the most uber woke zealots, there are now over seventy genders. It has now even got to the stage that many people including politicians, will not actually define what a woman is! This is usually so as to not cause any 'offence' and potentially lose votes in any upcoming elections, if they happen to represent a more left leaning, political party. And far worse: these militants want to spread their harmful ideologies and doctrines to the youngest of school age children as young as four to six years old, with drag queens being invited to their classrooms and reading out sexualised 'storybooks', telling boys they can be girls if they 'feel' that way and vice versa. All of this done in the so-called name of 'progress.' You have to ask yourself, when will this absolute madness end? The vast majority of the general public in western nations, regardless of their political and religious beliefs, or none, do not wish to see their children and grandchildren to be indoctrinated with such harmful content.

> Woe unto them that call evil good, and good evil; that put darkness for light, and light for darkness; that put bitter for sweet, and sweet for bitter! – (Isaiah 5:20 KJV.)

These warped and dangerous ideologies, could indeed, push whole new generations of disenfranchised and angry, young men, born after the September 2001 terror attacks on the World Trade Center and The Pentagon, towards extremist, Islamic movements and others into the extreme far right, if we do not get to grips with what is happening, all around us. It is also tragically sad, that more members of the LGBT community, who are themselves, against the militants within their own ranks, will be placed at further risk from violence, (and potential death) with many of those who live in more religiously strict, hard-line countries, where all forms of homosexuality are illegal, not being able to report their attacks to the authorities.

The fallout from the worst aspects of the manosphere movement – from incels, such as Elliott Rodger and Jake Davison, as terrible as they most certainly are, completely pale in comparison to the fallout that has come from the worst aspects, brought on by modern feminism. The evidence seen from the last half century at this time of writing is truly overwhelming: Industrial scale abortion, more family breakdown, separations and divorces, increased mental health issues and suicide rates among both sexes, damaged children and teenagers. Countless, young men who were brought up in chaotic, single parent households and were without decent, male role models, who all ended up being behind bars and/ or killed. Lack of respect towards others, especially in regards towards those with differing opinions, a sense of entitlement, ghastly ideologies from militant, woke elements, fast creeping into our schools, colleges, institutions, organisations, businesses, while trying their utmost to erode centuries of Judeo-Christian values, tradition and culture, and so much more.

Some may view the culture wars as being 'left vs right' but it is in fact, good vs evil. I truly hope and pray that as many people as possible, will renounce these destructive ideologies. And I also hope and pray, that as many people as possible, men and women, will turn to the one who can give us true peace and meaning in life. He may not be a muscular and heavily tattooed figure. He may not drive powerful sports cars and smoke Cuban cigars. He may not wear designer clothes and live in big houses in which he hosts, lively parties, anywhere in the world. He is a King but is also as humble as a servant.

His name is Jesus: who treats and views all men and women in equal measure. The one and only, true, supreme gentleman, that there ever has been or ever will be. Even the very best of advice given by the biggest names in the manosphere, cannot bring anyone, everlasting peace. Nor can it get you into Heaven. Renounce your sinful ways. Turn to Jesus, as soon as possible and without delay.

> Jesus Christ the same yesterday, and to day, and for ever. (Hebrews. 13:8 KJV.)

EXTRA: BECOMING
A CHRISTIAN

"Go on – Try it! Go on. You might get hit by a bus tomorrow."

Have you ever had anyone say this to you before? They may be urging you to try something new. It can range from anything, from a type of sauce to trying out a new recipe or to even something much less healthy, such as trying a shot of whiskey or the puff of a cigarette. And you may well indeed, get hit by a bus tomorrow....Or a car, or a truck, or a van or a motorbike. You may even get hit by any of the following, before tomorrow even arrives. Our very lives can be taken away from us at any given moment, via so many different ways, such as natural disasters, industrial accidents and even accidents within the confines of our own homes. At current, global levels, around 150,000 people die across the world, every single day. That is more than the population of Exeter, in south west England. Among that number, will be a fair percentage of people who will very sadly, never reach their fiftieth birthday. Whatever the case may be, we will all have to leave this life eventually, as over one-hundred billion people have already done so, throughout the entire course of human history. After life on Earth, there is just one of two places we can end up: Heaven and Hell. And both last for eternity. Hell, as was described by Jesus, is a place that you would not wish to spend just ten seconds in, let alone eternity!

And shall cast them into the furnace of fire: there shall be wailing and gnashing of teeth. (Matthew 13:50 KJV.)

To put it simply: it would be far easier to spend a whole year, locked up in one of the harshest prisons on Earth, than it would be to spend a single day in Hell. Those who willingly reject God, will ultimately be rejected by him too. Anyone who enters the gates of Hell, will never escape, and will spend a truly horrifying eternity, while also being among the company of unrepentant murderers, rapists, child molesters, those who tortured, maimed and killed others in the cruellest ways imaginable, and the worst ever, bloodthirsty tyrants, known in history.

> And whosoever was not found written
> in the book of life was cast into the lake
> of fire. – (Revelation. 20:15 KJV.)

Jesus Christ is THE way to Heaven!

It is for this reason, that Hell is mentioned so very frequently in both the Old and New Testament, to warn everyone during their time on Earth to avoid going there. We cannot enter Heaven, via our own deeds and 'good works', no matter how honest and well intentioned, that they may be. Ever since Adam and Eve brought sin into the world by disobeying God, all following generations and countless billions, throughout the ages, have encountered and suffered violence, greed, war, turmoil and despair, which very sadly, continues to this very day. Sin brought shame and separation between man and Almighty God. Only by the sacrifice of Jesus upon the cross, can that separation be bridged and can we then, have a true relationship with our Heavenly Father.

> "For God so loved the world that he gave his only begotten Son, that whosoever believeth in him should not perish but have everlasting life." (John 3:16 KJV.)

All that God asks, is that you turn to him, acknowledge your sin, ask for forgiveness and ask that Jesus enters your life.

> "Jesus saith unto him. I am the way, the truth and the life: no man cometh unto the Father but by me." (John 14:6 KJV.)

To become a Christian, please pray the following:

"Dear Lord, Heavenly Father, I acknowledge that I am a sinner and have fallen completely short of your standards. I recognise that Jesus paid the ultimate price for my sins and shed his blood for me, upon the cross. Please forgive me and to ask for Jesus to enter into my heart, to cleanse me of my sin and for the Holy Spirit to transform and renew my life. This, I ask, in Jesus mighty name. Amen."

If you have said this prayer and truly meant it, then congratulations: You are now a Christian. This does not mean that your life on this Earth will be a bed of roses, each and every day, but you can be rest assured of salvation and the hope of glorious, eternal life with the Lord of the Universe. You may wish to take a few moments to reflect on this, the best decision that you could ever make in your lifetime, and to thank God, once again, shortly after your conversion. Tell someone very dear to you, about your decision to turn to Christ. Try to meet other Christians, as soon as it is possible to do so and settle into a church in your area. You may wish to visit several, before deciding which one will be the right one for you. Take care and God bless. Wishing you the very best on your journey.

Printed in the United States
by Baker & Taylor Publisher Services